23

Varieties of Ethnic Art

and how to make each one

23

Varieties of Ethnic Art

and how to make each one

written by Jean and Cle Kinney

Atheneum   1976   New York

Library of Congress Cataloging in Publication Data
Kinney, Jean Brown.
23 varieties of ethnic art
and how to make each one.

SUMMARY: Explains the contributions to American
culture of many different ethnic groups and
provides instructions for making
folk art for each group.
1. Handicraft—Juvenile literature.
2. Folk art—Juvenile literature.
[1. Folk art. 2. Handicraft. 3. United States—
Foreign population] I. Kinney, Cle, joint author. II. Title.
TT160.K48   745.5   76-5409
ISBN 0-689-30541-9

Published simultaneously in Canada by
McClelland & Stewart, Ltd.
Manufactured in the United States of America by
Halliday Lithograph Corporation
West Hanover, Massachusetts
Typography designed by Nora Sheehan
First Edition

CONTENTS

3 | NEW INTEREST IN OLD WAYS

FIVE WAYS TO
USE THIS BOOK

AN ETHNIC GROUP is one in which members belong to the same race or nationality and have common traits and customs. In this book, you will see art objects made by members of twenty-three ethnic groups. As you look at the work and learn how to do it, you will learn about people who have contributed to the culture of the United States, either because they have come to live here or their crafts have been valued here.

To get the most out of this book, use it these five ways.

1. **Go straight through the book, looking at all the pictures.**
   In a few minutes, you will see that this country is unlike other countries in that it has taken people and ideas from many different countries.

   When you read the book, you will find out how the Spaniards came, found gold and took it back to their king who made coins out of it. You will discover that the English came and settled in houses with neat hedges where their aim was to live as they had lived at home. You will see the tulips, hearts and flowers the Pennsylvania Germans put on their furniture and plates, the great papier-maché figures the French made (and still make) for their carnival that comes before Lent, the woven tartans made by the Scotch. You will see woodcarvings made by slaves brought here against their will from Africa and engravings made by Eskimos who have lived in our northland for centuries and jewelry made by Indians.

2. With the help of this map, see where many of the groups whose folk art has influenced America came from.

On the map below, you will find numbered circles in twenty-three places. Each number corresponds with a chapter's number in PART II. (Number 1 on the map of Spain corresponds with chapter 1 on page 13, which is about people from Spain.) Each numbered country is the place where one of the groups in this book lives or did live. As you read about a group and its art, look back at the map and find the number on the map that corresponds with the number of the chapter you are reading. Then, you will know the homeland of that group.

1	SPAIN
2	ENGLAND
3	HOLLAND
4	AFRICA
5	GERMANY
6	FRANCE
7	ISRAEL
8	SCOTLAND
9	IRELAND
10	ITALY
11	GERMANY
12	CZECHOSLOVAKIA
13	SCANDINAVIA
14	UKRAINE
15	SWITZERLAND
16	CANADA
17	ALASKA
18	AMERICAN SOUTHWEST
19	JAVA
20	JAPAN
21	CHINA
22	MOROCCO
23	MEXICO

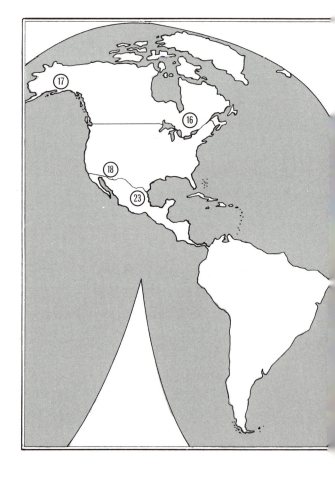

3. Look at the art and get to know the people.

As you look at Dutch tiles made in Holland and later in New Amsterdam, which was the first name for New York, you will see pictures of boats, windmills, fishermen and boys on skates. So you will know that the people who made these tiles lived near water. Look at the clocks made in the Amana colonies, and you will know that the Germans who worked on them are patient, hard-working people. Look at the piñatas from Mexico filled with candy and toys, and you will know that Mexicans who make them love color and excitement. Most art objects have something to say about their makers.

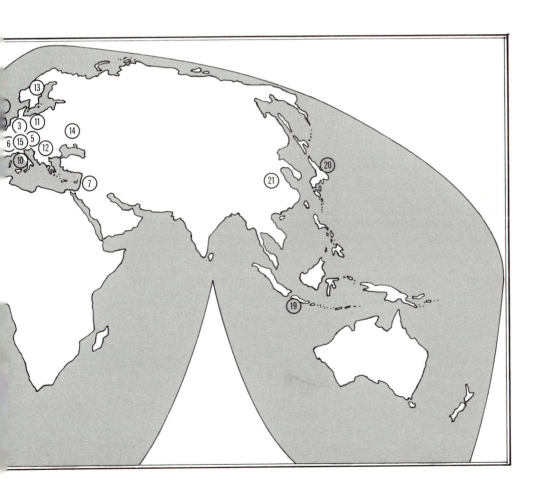

4. Find where your grandparents came from and learn more about yourself.

Did your parents, grandparents or ancestors before them come from Ireland, Switzerland, Czechoslovakia or Italy? Or from Africa, China or Ukraine? Or from another of the countries numbered on the map? Read about how they lived and what they made with their hands.

By reading about the ethnic group or groups you belong to, you will get a better understanding of your parents and grandparents and begin to see why you think and work as you do. In so doing, you may come to know yourself better.

5. Do some experimenting to discover your talents.

If your ancestors came from Ireland, where many have a gift for words, see if you too have this same gift. Write something—a poem, an essay or a story. Or if your ancestors came from Italy, where many through the ages have worked with stone, make a mosaic or a carving or build a stone wall. You will see as you work whether the gift has come down to you. If you think not, go through the book and find another kind of art work that interests you. Make *something*! As you work, you will find your talent.

1

ART BY AMERICANS
WITH DIFFERENT
BEGINNINGS

Since 1886, the Statue of Liberty, standing on Liberty Island in New York harbor, has welcomed ethnic groups to this country with the promise of freedom. In her hand, the woman who is 150 feet high, holds a lighted torch. She was made by French sculptor, Frédéric A. Bartholdi and paid for by the people of France who admired America's dedication to liberty for all.

Old Customs
in a New Country

WHEN A GROUP from another country becomes part of this one, the newcomers do not immediately give up their old customs. They cook as they have cooked for years, do the dances they danced before, play games they played as children and speak as they learned long ago. Sometimes, they have celebrations on days that were holidays where they used to live. The Irish celebrate St. Patrick's Day, the French have a Mardi Gras, the Swiss remember William Tell. The celebrations preserve tradition and help newcomers to feel less homesick, and they also make America a more exciting place to live.

Dancing the Highland Fling.

Breaking a Mexican piñata.

Doing a Hawaiian dance.

As a boy in Iowa's Amana Colonies, Harry Zuber liked to work with his hands. He learned how to carve wooden furniture from older relatives and friends whose German grandparents had settled in nearby villages. Now, he makes duck decoys and doll furniture in his own home.

Handed-Down Skills
from Faraway Places

GERMAN CHILDREN whose parents make things with their hands learn to do the same. So do Italian children and African children and Jewish children. So do children everywhere.

America is filled with people whose parents and grandparents from another country were taught to work in a special way with materials close at hand. Today, these people make handmade quilts, paintings, mosaics, carvings and other beautiful things. Sometimes, they use materials they didn't have in their old country, but they work with methods handed down from long ago. Later, they will hand the old methods down to their children, and the art will go on.

Weaving is popular in North Carolina, settled by Scots.

Carving is the art of Idaho Basques (from southern France and Spain).

Calendar in Zoar, Ohio, was made by Germans in 1817.

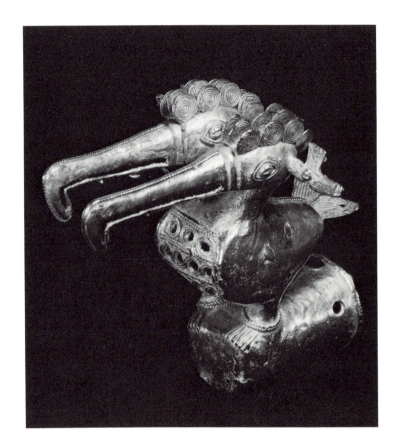

This two-headed gold pelican was made by Indians in South America about the time that Columbus was discovering America. Many gold objects like this were melted down by Spanish explorers, but a few remain.

Handmade Things from
Way Back When

ARTISTS WITH GREAT natural talent can produce impressive works of art even when they have had no formal training.

The double-headed bird with ears, wings and two long beaks was made of hammered gold by an unknown native of Colombia, South America, between 1000 and 1600 A.D., which was centuries before newcomers to this continent could make anything this complicated. The carved figure at the right with the bulging eyes was photographed in Georgia in 1940 and is thought to be the work of the uneducated descendant of a slave from Africa. And the three totem figures were carved by Indians in Alaska. Made out of a giant cedar tree, the three figures originally were not separate, but carved into a giant, one-piece tribal monument.

Totem figures
by Alaskan Indians

Bust by self-trained
carver.

Carvings found in Alaska in the
1800s thought to have been done by
Chinese sailors on an Arctic voyage.

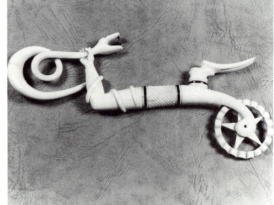

Carving (scrimshaw) by American
sailor has pastry crimper and pie-
testing fork opposite arm with writh-
snake.

Several Ways of Handling
the Same Material

THE THREE CARVINGS shown here were made out of ivory that began as a tooth (either of a whale or a walrus). For each one, the artist cut out a figure and, then, cut into the figure. But there, any likeness ends.

The arm with the snake is a kitchen tool made by a man on a whaling vessel for his mother or wife back home. The statues, made on a Chinese boat have Oriental feeling. And the walrus, made by an Eskimo, was carved by someone who knew this animal well. So here you have three artists working with ivory whose carvings are different because their backgrounds were different. Probably if you do a carving in ivory or anything else, your work will be nothing like one of these.

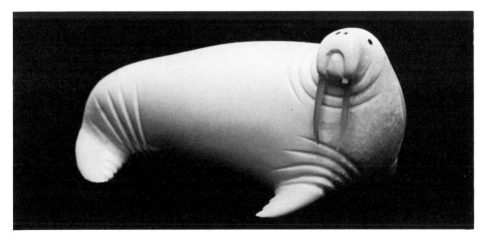

Carving by an Eskimo who knows the walrus well.

As New Ones Come,
the Arts Go On

GROUPS FROM EVERY country have come to the United States to worship and live as they want. With them they have brought their arts. And in some cases, folk arts have come by themselves, the groups of the people who made them have not come at all. But as all these arts are seen, others, not of that ethnic group, copy the designs or the methods, and so the art goes on and grows.

In Chinatown on New York's Lower East Side, for example, small shops display rare objects to customers who are not Chinese. They see new ways to make screens, carve ivory and paint on silk. So, methods used in a faraway country become known to people from another. And out of this new arts can develop.

2

23 VARIETIES OF ETHNIC ART AND HOW TO MAKE EACH ONE

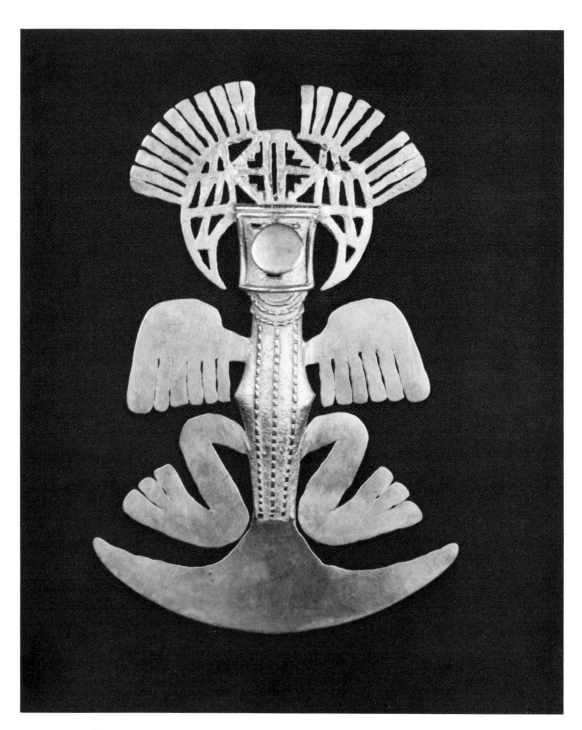

This golden god was made by Indians in South America. Along with shiploads of gold and silver, such treasures were sent to Spain by conquistadores. Most were melted down.

Gold: Found and Worked
by the Spanish

SPANIARDS WHO FOLLOWED Columbus to the colony he founded at Hispaniola (Haiti) mined gold on this island and the mainland. They sent shiploads of gold and silver back to Spain, and there expert metalsmiths turned the precious metals into crowns, church ornaments, jewelry and coins.

Unfortunately, Spaniards, who respected great metalwork at home, did not understand the art objects hammered or cast out of gold by

King's golden crown
(*654* A.D.).

Church masterpiece
(*early 1500s*).

Spanish coin (*made after
the time of Columbus*).

This crown was made by the Chavin Indians of Peru who lived before the time of Christ. It is made of gold that has been hammered into a thin sheet and shaped. Decorations are bulging (embossed) heads of gods.

the Indians. So they melted down the crowns and pendants they found and sent the bouillion home. This was a boon to Spanish metalsmiths, but it robbed this country of priceless art objects. Only a few pieces found in graves and hidden places are still around.

Achieving the Look of Hammered Gold

A smooth crown from the late Stone Age has been found in Spain's Cave of the Bats. For this, the gold apparently was worked into a sheet by being hammered on a stone;.then it was trimmed with a sharp stone and bent into shape. Ornaments made later had raised surface designs made by hammering a gold sheet on the reverse side.

You can achieve the look of hammered gold on 36-gauge copper foil. Along with your foil, you will need tracing paper, pencil, masking tape, steel modeler, wooden spoon, table knife, art metal fill, steel wool and liquid liver of sulphur or stain. You can make the sun as shown on the this page or anything else.

Once you get the knack of working with copper sheeting, you can make monograms, profile drawings of children and decorative overlays for boxes, bookends, coasters, trays and other household objects.

have made a simple drawing, to copper sheet and place on cardboard or cutting board. Using a sharp pencil, transfer to copper by tracing over drawing.

2. Turn copper reverse side up and place on pad of newspapers. With steel modeler, make bulges you want on other side. In the sun shown here, the nose, lips, cheeks and streaks in rays will bulge.

3. Now turn the sheet over, and with the same modeler press down what you want to indent. Work the tool back and forth, being careful not to stretch the copper beyond its ability to "give."

4. On back side fill pressed places with art metal fill, using a table knife as shown here. Let fill dry till hard and turn again to front side.

5. Antique your work with liquid liver of sulphur or stain, working into depressions. Or for a translucent effect, work color into your design with a felt color pen.

6. When finish is dry, polish design with steel wool. Apply clear lacquer and mount your work on wooden panel with tacks or glue to heavy cardboard. Frame as a picture, if desired.

This twenty-foot topiary giraffe, grown from privet (a shrub), is sixty years old. It lives at Green Animals Park at Portsmouth, Rhode Island, near Newport. Nearby are a topiary bear, swan, goat, horse and rider, camel and elephant.

From the English, Topiary Art

ROMAN GARDENS had shrubs and trees cut in ornamental shapes, but this topiary work did not become an art form until it was perfected by English gardeners in the sixteenth century. In this country, through the eighteenth century, gardeners for American estates, owned by people whose ancestors were English, had walls, dividers, borders and spirals carved from privet, yew and other shrubbery.

Later, Americans came to prefer more natural-looking gardens, and many of the ornamental shrubs were cut down. But now, at places like Mount Vernon and Williamsburg, the gardens have been restored. And artists in other places as well are creating topiary animals. With patience, string and a clipping shears, you can do the same.

George Washington's garden at
Mount Vernon.

Topiary fantasy preserved in
Rhode Island.

This camel has four privet legs for support. The young wood was bent to grow into this shape and tied. The camel developed in five years.

This poodle has an inner frame of chicken wire. Ivy growing from potting soil within the frame (lined with damp sheet moss) gives curly look.

Easy way to grow a topiary animal

You can grow your ivy from within an animal-shaped frame as described above. Or you can twist long strands of ivy around a silhouette type animal frame set in a pot. Find the step-by-step directions for this easy second method on the next page.

For the rabbit shown here, you will need three coat hangers, wire cutter, tape, one large pot of ivy with long strands, one pair shears. With your first coat hanger, make a silhouette of a rabbit's head with long ears. With your second, make the lower half of the body and feet; and with the third, make the back and tail. "Crimp" parts together and bind with tape. "Plant" frame in pot, and entwine strands of ivy around frame, and, soon you will have a rabbit with a healthy green coat.

1. Molding head. Bend your first hanger into the shape of a rabbit's head with long ears. Clip off hook with wire cutter.

2. Bend (and clip) your second hanger into the shape of the lower half of a rabbit's body with two pairs of legs. Tape and crimp to head.

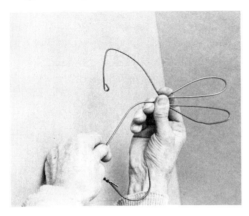

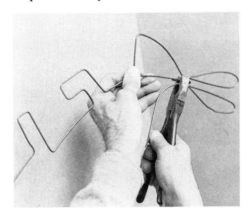

3. Bend, clip and crimp upper back of rabbit to head and lower half as shown. Tape parts together.

4. "Plant" frame in pot of ivy, as shown.

5. Entwine ivy loosely through and around frame to fill out body of rabbit.

6. Prune away leaves which take away from rabbit's silhouette.

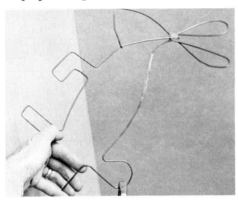

These tiles are typical of those made in Holland in the seventeenth century when Dutch art was at its best. Each has a blue figure set against a gleaming white background. Designed at Delft by artists, such tiles brightened homes in Holland and in America, where the Dutch had settled at New Amsterdam, which later became New York.

From the Dutch,
Tile Making as an Art

THREE CENTURIES AGO in Holland, where it rains often, the Dutch were using rows of tiles as baseboards in their cottages to resist damnpess (and in fireplaces to withstand soot damage). And they were putting shining white tiles on the walls for decoration as we put up pictures. In Delft, where tile making became an art, artists worked out designs for tile makers who hired unknown workers to copy the pictures and do the actual finishing. So painters influenced tile making and tile makers influenced painters. One great painter, Johannes Vermeer, who lived from 1632 to 1675, selected colors for his paintings (white, blue and light yellow) that were identical to those being used by tile makers.

The Dutch, who were shipbuilders and traders, exported their tiles to Germany, Denmark, Spain, Java and especially to America. Here,

Vermeer's painting, *The Cook*, with its woman at work in a whitewashed kitchen, has the look of a tile made in the seventeenth century, when Holland produced its best tiles and paintings.

Even the most humble homes in Holland have tiles on the walls and fireplace to resist dampness and soot damage, as well as for decoration.

beautiful tiles went up on the walls of Dutch houses or were used on the hearth as "fireplace stones." Most tiles had a picture of a flower, a man or a woman at work, a child at play or a boat or ship of some sort. Usually, the central drawing was blue and was painted on white clay. The whole was covered with a shining glaze.

How to make a 6-inch square tile without a kiln

Using a new cellulose-base product available at craft shops, you can make a square tile without a kiln, to hang on your wall or to use under a hot dish or put on your table. Here is all you need.

Two standard ¾ inch wooden stripes 12 inches long, which you can buy at any lumber yard
Four ½ inch nails
Old board or table top
Ruler
Rolling pin or round bottle
One package of Sculptamold
Water

Coarse sandpaper
Mixing bowl
6-inch square of cork or felt for backing
Glue
Small paintbrush
Blue acrylic paint
Artist's fine brush

1. Nail two ¾-inch wooden strips, six inches apart, on old board or table top. Place wax paper on board.

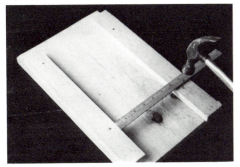

2. Make "mud pie" of two parts Sculptamold and one part water. Place between strips.

3. Roll out Sculptamold with rolling pin or round bottle (riding on strips for uniform thickness).

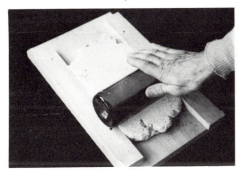

4. Cut away excess "dough" to make 6-inch square tile. Let stand for several days or bake in 200° oven until dry. Sand when dry.

5. Draw design and corner decorations on tile. Fill in blue acrylic paint with fine brush.

6. Varnish top and sides. Glue felt or cork to bottom of tile as table protector.

This unusual carving, known as *Boy with a Bucket*, was presented to the owner of a water-powered grist mill in Fayetteville, New York, when a daughter was born in 1842. The artist is unknown, but the carving has an African feeling and probably was made by a black millworker. The figure is eight inches tall and carved in one piece out of soft pine.

Woodcarving by Slaves from Africa

IN 1619, A YEAR before the Pilgrims landed at Plymouth, twenty blacks were sold into slavery in Virginia by the owner of a Dutch ship who had captured them from the Spanish. From then until the Civil War, blacks were bought and sold in America. Along the way, a few northern slaves were freed, and laws were passed that prevented the buying of new slaves from overseas. Still by 1863, when President Lincoln issued his Emancipation Proclamation, close to four million men, women and children were owned, largely by farmers and plantation owners.

Most of America's slaves were descendants of blacks from Africa, where woodcarving is popular. These Americans had no money for brushes, paint and other art materials, but they could make woodcarvings because wood is plentiful here. They did not carve the masks and figures that are carved for religious reasons in Africa, however. Instead they made wooden furniture and tools for their masters and their cabins. And they carved likenesses of snakes, chickens, other animals and men, and made dolls like this one, which is chiseled out of walnut and looks like George Washington.

In Africa, headdresses like this carved ram's head, and figures and masks by skillful artists serve a purpose at religious ceremonies and social gatherings. In America, slaves from Africa were introduced to a new religion and tended to carve crosses and figures associated with Christianity rather than carvings of this kind. Many of these were used as grave markers in cemeteries.

Much "graveyard art" made by blacks is now in museums, but here
are two pieces photographed in an old cemetery in Georgia. Usually,
blacks made their carvings in one piece. The animal sculpture here
is an exception. The head and body were carved separately and
fitted together.

Chickens, animals, snakes and men became subjects for black artists who worked with knife, adze or chisel on found wood. Note how the grain of the wood here suggests the feathers of the chicken.

This frog, photographed in 1940 by Malcolm Bell of Savannah, is carved from small wooden block.

Mixing spoon with ornate handle was found in slave quarters of old hotel in the South.

Canes and walking sticks were decorated with snakes carved into the wood. Sometimes, the snakes were painted in bright colors. Musical instruments were hand-carved, too. The banjo, believed to have been invented by the American black slave, has a neck of carved wood fastened to a "head" made of skin stretched over a round hoop.

Here are four walking sticks and one figure. The walking sticks were all carved from saplings or ordinary sticks. The figure, which may have been designed as a cane head, was probably cut from a short length of freshly cut timber. Note how the knobs and bulges on each stick have been worked into the design.

How to make a walking stick

If you live near a woods, find a small pine, poplar, birch or basswood sapling, or branch that will yield a 30-inch stick. (The sapling should be about 1½ inches thick before peeling.) Peel away bark and examine stick for lumps and markings that you can work into your design. Draw your overall design on the stick.

No sapling? Look for a dead branch after a storm or for driftwood on the beach, or get a 30-inch length of clear pine (¾-inch square) at your lumberyard. In such cases, draw on the wood as is.

With a jackknife whittle away excess wood to bring out your design. (Let your snake, turtle or head stand out in relief.) Keep your cutting edge sharp. Work with the grain, and cut away from your body. Smooth your carved stick with sandpaper and let it weather naturally. Protect with shellac or varnish, if you want.

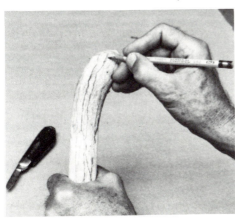

Draw your design on peeled branch or dead wood.

Carve away excess wood to bring out design.

Tulips, birds and hearts were worked into German fractur, which combines large angular letters with color decorations. Introduced into America by Protestant refugees from the Rhineland, it was popular from the late 1600s through the middle 1800s. Masters of the art were German schoolteachers who drew up certificates of baptism and marriage.

Tulips, Hearts and Hex Signs
by the Pennsylvania Dutch

T HE PEOPLE KNOWN as Pennsylvania Dutch who settled in large numbers near Lancaster and Reading were not Dutch. The name came because they talked of *Deutschland*, which is the German word for Germany. In the beginning, they came from the Palatinate, an area of what is now Germany, at the invitation of William Penn. These Protestant Germans, who came to Pennsylvania by the thousands in the 1700s, worked hard. They were deeply religious and kept alive their Old World traditions, but they enjoyed life, too. As they prospered, they brightened their furniture, pottery, coverlets and books with tulips, hearts and peacocks.

Plain and Fancy—that's the way the Pennsylvania Dutch break down today. The plain people are the Mennonites, Amish and Dunkers who

Flowers were painted on blanket chests.

Tulips were scratched through slip on plates.

WELCOME　　　　　　　　　　GOOD LUCK

travel in horse and buggies, shun farm machinery and wear beards and buttonless clothes. The "fancy" Pennsylvania Dutch are churchgoers and loyal to the past, but modern in their ways. The Pennsylvania Germans still appreciate good food and know how to grow and prepare it. And they are still proud of these popular forms of Pennsylvania folk art which you can adapt:

Fractur—(meaning *break*) is the calligraphy (writing) popular in Germany in the Middle Ages. (See page 30.) It calls for careful writing with a pen and painting with a brush. Plan your work carefully and plot out lightly with a pencil before you start lettering with a pen or painting with a brush.

Hand-decorated furniture—brightened with tulips, peacocks and hearts. The familiar decorations can be transferred to chests, bureaus, chairs, wooden trays, flowerpots and tinware. To apply a design to an unpainted (or stripped) piece of furniture or to wood for a wall plaque, smooth wood with sandpaper, and then paint with white acrylic paint for background. Trace or draw on a simple design and fill in pattern with acrylic paint in red, yellow, green and blue or other colors. Glaze with raw umber glaze, if desired. Follow the same procedure when painting a clay pot, making sure pot is clean and dry when you begin. For tinware, remove all traces of rust with steel wool and then rinse ware clean with solution of 50 percent vinegar and 50 percent water. Let dry and proceed as for wood.

All through Pennsylvania, you will see hex signs painted by Jacob Zook, Paradise, Pennsylvania's "hex man." A twelfth generation Pennsylvania Dutchman, Mr. Zook knows what signs ward off bad luck and bring good luck. Every year, he produces and ships 120,000 hex signs similar to the two pictured.

How to make a hex sign

Even if you're not superstitious, design an attractive hex sign for your front door or family room. Study Mr. Zook's symbols below for an inspiration. Then, when you have designed a hex sign with a special meaning for you, cover a circle of masonite (at least 12 inches in circumference) with white acrylic paint. When dry, paint on your design in red, green, black and yellow. Varnish your sign if you are hanging it outdoors. Hang with nail through a center hole.

Rosette for joy

Eagle for strength

Four Seasons for prosperity

Starburst to get your wish

No papier-maché figures anywhere are as elaborate as the ones that parade each year at the Mardi Gras carnival in the old French quarter of New Orleans. With the help of inner mechanisms, papier-maché animals toss their heads, roll their eyes, twitch their tails and even belch steam as the giant lizard is doing here.

Paper-Maché
by the French

PAPIER-MACHÉ is paper mush mixed with glue. When the mushy material is dried on or in a mold, it holds the shape of that mold. In the 1600s, papier-maché was used in France and other European countries for the making of boxes and trays that eventually found their way to America.

Nowhere is papier-maché used more creatively than in New Orleans. And at no event are there as many papier-maché figures as at the city's annual Mardi Gras celebration, which got its start in America in 1699. That year, on the Tuesday before Ash Wednesday, a few homesick French explorers stopped beside a stream and remembered the celebrating done by Catholics in France on that day. They named the stream Mardi Gras, which means Fat Tuesday. Soon after, French settlers in Louisiana began to celebrate Fat Tuesday with parades and a ball. Merrymaking at a pre-Lenten carnival became an annual event and continued even after Napoleon sold the Louisiana Territory to the United States. Today, the New Orleans Mardi Gras attracts thousands of visitors every year.

Each year, the Mardi Gras kings ride on enormous papier-maché floats.

Huge crowds watch one giant papier-maché float after another make its way through the old streets of New Orleans in parades that go on for several days before Lent. And a fortunate few go to the grand balls at which each year's Mardi Gras king and queen for the various social clubs are announced. Others see the brilliant gem-studded costumes worn by each year's royalty on giant and/or life-size papier-maché figures at Mardi Gras World in the colorful French Quarter of the old Louisiana city and at the Louisiana State Museum.

Hit of the 1975 Mardi Gras in New Orleans was this great white papier-maché bull on a float decorated with cornucopias out of which tumbled papier-maché grapes, pears and other fruit.

Recipe for Papier-Maché

Stack of large-size newspapers   *4 cups water*
1½ cups of flour   *1 bucket—empty*
½ cup Elmer's glue   *1 bucket—filled with water*

In 1 bucket (empty), mix water, flour and glue to a thin paste. Tear double page of newspaper the long way into strips. Shuffle these long strips in the clear water in the other bucket.

Now, put moistened strips into bucket containing paste. Take out two or three or more strips at a time and mush (or layer) these strips together to make the papier-maché.

How to make a papier-maché head with chicken wire, glued strips and waterproof paint

1. Make a drawing of how you want your head to look. (Select model from a book or create an original.)

2. Using chicken wire, make a wire foundation for your head. (Leave room at the neck to insert your own head later.)

3. Place layered strips of moist, glued paper on wire until frame is completely covered.

4. Build up nose, cheeks, eyebrows, lips with crumpled pieces of wet, glued paper.

5. When head is dry, paint with white latex or acrylic paint.

6. With acrylic, or any other waterproof paint, paint face and features on head.

In Germany in 1800, the unicorn and the Hebrew inscription in the seal at the top of this picture was engraved in a carnelian, which is a reddish variety of quartz. Directly below is an imprint made by pressing the engraved seal in hot wax, lead or some other molten material. (And below that is a second impression from the same engraved seal.) Note how the unicorn at the top is cut *into* the stone and the inscription is written in reverse "mirror writing." In both impressions below the seal the unicorn *stands out in relief* and the Hebrew inscription can be read as Arich Zuee, Son of Jacob Einhorn. Einhorn means "unicorn."

From Ancient Times,
Engraving of Seals by Jews

IN ANCIENT TIMES, men paid taxes in the form of products. Instead of sending money to the king's treasurer, they sent jars of honey or oil or bales of grain. To get proper credit, they put a special mark on each jar and bale. To do the stamping on terra cotta jar handles or baled grain, they needed a seal, so they went to a seal cutter.

Seal cutters made seals for traders, merchants, noblemen and priests as well as farmers. They made many religious amulets also, which had a signature and a hole for a thong that tied the amulet to the owner's wrist or around his neck. One seal maker (Beseleel) in Palestine, where cutting gems was a fine art, is mentioned in the Old Testament, Exodus 35:30; the account tells us the Lord filled Beseleel with knowledge in the cutting of stones . . . "to set them, and to make any manner of cunning work."

The ancient piece below tells the story of Abraham, who learned through obedience that "the Lord will provide." As Abraham, Isaac's father, raises his knife to sacrifice the life of his beloved son, as he believes God has willed, he sees the hand of God pointing to a ram caught

The pitcher on this ring was carved in wax and then cast in silver. It is the symbol of the Levites who were aides for the Cohanim, the priestly caste. The signature is that of Solomon, son of Uriel Levi.

under a small tree to indicate that Abraham could sacrifice the ram, not his son. On the reverse side are indistinct letters of a Semetic alphabet believed to be Hebrew.

In Germany in the seventeenth and eighteenth centuries, Jews went from seal cutting to medal casting and became better than all others at this. And in America, they went from seal cutting to miniature painting at which they excelled.

Through the centuries, scribes became interpreters for traders and served as their treasurers. Thus, they came to know the ways of trading, and many became traders or bankers. Others became coin makers, and a few seal cutters, who were gifted artists, went from seal making to other branches of art.

During the great years of European art, when the churches did most of the hiring of painters and sculptors, few opportunities came to Jews. There were three reasons for this: (1) Work commissioned by the churches often had to do with the New Testament. So, because Jewish religion is concerned with the Old Testament, this automatically cut off the Jewish artist. (2) The Jewish religion forbids making a graven (firmly fixed) likeness of God. And, last (and probably the most important), as Christianity spread, prejudice against Jews became strong, and the churches used any excuse not to hire Jewish painters and sculptors. So Jewish artists concentrated on those branches of art where their religion was not questioned—seal cutting and gem engraving.

Now that art is commissioned by others besides the church and is concerned with subjects other than religion, Jewish artists have become painters and sculptors and have contributed much to all branches of art.

The Art of Seal Making

The engraving of stones for seals and jewelry is called glyptic art. This comes from the Greek word, *glyptos*, which means *carved*. And any seal or gem with a design cut into the stone is called intaglio. This comes from the Italian word, *intagliere*, which means *to cut in*.

The first seals were cut into soft stone with a bird bone, shell or flint chip. Engraved in such stones are fish, boats, animals and grain. Later, seals were cut into hard stones (held firm in pitch) with a metal-tipped bow drill. These seals have engravings of houses and family symbols. With the seal, an impression could be made in clay or wax, or a mark could be put on paper.

Seal cutting in hard stone calls for a pitch block or vise, sand, water and a sharp revolving drill. The process is complicated, but below is an easy way to make a seal that you can use to make an impression in sealing wax. All you will need are Sculptamold, which you can buy at a craft store, sandpaper, a sharp knife, a stick of sealing wax and a candle.

1. Roll prepared Sculptamold into "jelly roll" stick. Cut off one end.

2. Let dry, and smooth cut end of "jelly roll" by rubbing on sandpaper.

3. With sharp knife, carve symbol or initial (in reverse) in smooth end of roll. Shellac.

4. Soften stick of sealing wax over lighted candle.

5. Daub softened sealing wax on flap of unsealed envelope.

6. Press carved Sculptamold seal into hot wax to leave imprint.

This hammer thrower, dressed in a wraparound kilt, is competing in a weight event at the Grandfather Mountain Highland Games near Linville, North Carolina. Here, members of Scottish clans in the tartans (plaids) of their ancestors gather each summer to play Scottish games, listen to pipers and dance the Highland Fling. All march in the Parade of the Tartans.

The Weaving of Tartans
by the Scottish

MANY SCOTS IN North Carolina are descendants of Highlanders from northern Scotland. Back home, for centuries, each family belonged to a clan made up of people who were related to each other in some way. All members of each clan wanted to know on sight who would fight on their side in case of trouble. So all wore kilts or scarves woven in the same plaid pattern or tartan.

Each woven tartan was made from wool fibers that had been bleached white in the sun and/or colored red, green, blue, yellow or black with dyes from roots and berries. And each family kept count on a piece of wood of the number and colors of threads in their pattern. With this record, any weaver could make the tartan.

Farmers from Scotland raised sheep in the Carolina mountains as they had at home. And the women spun wool and wove coverlets and clothing. After the Civil War, mill owners moved south from New England with power looms, and, for a long time, weavers did not work much at home. Now hand-woven Scotch plaids are much admired, and the mountain people are weaving again.

A weaver at Penland, North Carolina, works at loom like those used by mountain people.

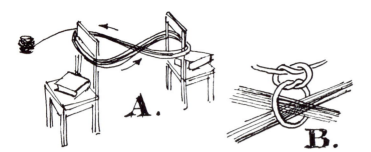

Put together a simple backstrap loom with materials in Rigid Heddle Loom Kit, which you can order from School Products, Inc., 1201 Broadway, New York City, 10001. The first time you weave, make a simple tie or sash.

How to make a plaid sash with a backstrap loom

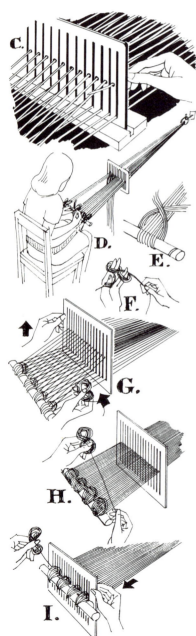

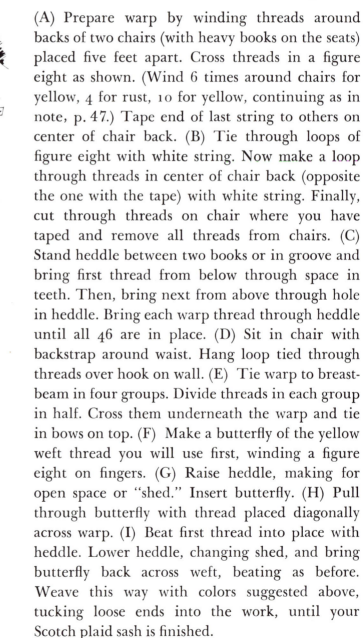

(A) Prepare warp by winding threads around backs of two chairs (with heavy books on the seats) placed five feet apart. Cross threads in a figure eight as shown. (Wind 6 times around chairs for yellow, 4 for rust, 10 for yellow, continuing as in note, p. 47.) Tape end of last string to others on center of chair back. (B) Tie through loops of figure eight with white string. Now make a loop through threads in center of chair back (opposite the one with the tape) with white string. Finally, cut through threads on chair where you have taped and remove all threads from chairs. (C) Stand heddle between two books or in groove and bring first thread from below through space in teeth. Then, bring next from above through hole in heddle. Bring each warp thread through heddle until all 46 are in place. (D) Sit in chair with backstrap around waist. Hang loop tied through threads over hook on wall. (E) Tie warp to breast-beam in four groups. Divide threads in each group in half. Cross them underneath the warp and tie in bows on top. (F) Make a butterfly of the yellow weft thread you will use first, winding a figure eight on fingers. (G) Raise heddle, making for open space or "shed." Insert butterfly. (H) Pull through butterfly with thread placed diagonally across warp. (I) Beat first thread into place with heddle. Lower heddle, changing shed, and bring butterfly back across weft, beating as before. Weave this way with colors suggested above, tucking loose ends into the work, until your Scotch plaid sash is finished.

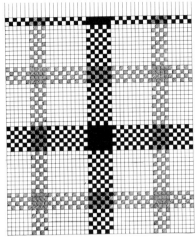

Note:

For a fringed plaid sash (3-1/2 inches wide, 60 inches long) in yellow, rust and blue, we strung warp threads of fine two-ply wool (as planned on graph paper) as follows: 6 yellow, 4 rust, 10 yellow, 6 blue, 10 yellow, 4 rust and 6 yellow. Then, we crisscrossed wth same colors in weft, as shown.

Or you may want to make hot mat or a coaster on a simple cardboard loom.

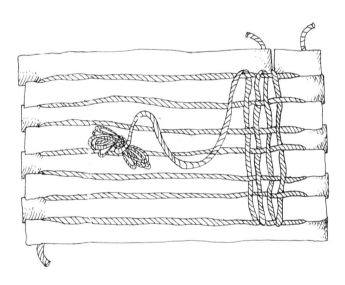

(1) Draw lines 1/2 inch apart on a piece of heavy cardboard 5 1/2 x 6 1/2 inches and cut in 1/2 inch along each line at both ends. (2) Use rug yarn, and thread the warp by fastening the yarn in the first slit at one end, then stretching it along the first line and through the first slit at the other end. Cross the yarn back of the cardboard and pass it through the second slit. Stretch it along the second line. Repeat for all ten lines. (3) Make a butterfly of the weft yarn as shown in the drawing for the backstrap loom and pass the butterfly over and under the warp. Push each row into place, making sure not to pull the yarn too tight. When you change color, begin opposite the side on which you ended and tuck the loose ends into the weaving. (4) To finish, sew along warp edges with needle and thread to keep from ravelling, or knot every two warp threads together to form a fringe. Cut loops. You may want to try making a wall hanging using a longer piece of cardboard. Insert dowels through the loops at either end of your work for hanging.

In 1912, the comic strip, *Bringing Up Father*, was created by a second generation Irishman named George McManus. The continuing story featured social-climbing Maggie, who had been a washerwoman, and her henpecked husband, Jiggs, who had struck it rich but longed for the good old days when he could eat corned beef and cabbage and didn't have to wear spats. This strip in the series, which earned its author more than $12 million, appeared during World War II.

Irish Wit
and Wordsmithing

IN THE THREE years before 1850, Ireland had a great famine. The potatoes that fed the country were afflicted by a blight, and half a million people starved to death. Up to then, about 35,000 Irish emigrants had been coming to America each year, but, now more than 200,000 came in one year alone. Soon, city slums overflowed with the half-starved Irish, many of whom could not read or write.

Even before the famine, the Irish were poor, as a whole, and most had almost no chance to go to school. So they arrived here without education or money. Still, they had three advantages over other new-comers. They spoke English. They had wit. And they had a gift for words. (Denied learning, they admired those who used words well and encouraged this talent in their children.) So the Irish here produced teachers, poets and storytellers in great numbers.

George McManus—In the early 1900s, George McManus, the Missouri-born son of two Irish emigrants, created a comic strip that captured the spirit of the American Irish. (Most wanted to be accepted socially

by their Protestant neighbors, but few wanted to give up their Irish ways and friends.) With Jiggs, a one-time hod carrier, his ridiculous wife, Maggie, and their lovely daughter, Nora, McManus had a believable family for all to laugh at and love.

The father of George McManus was manager of the St. Louis Opera House, and there, George saw a play about a newly rich Irish family starring the Irish actor, Billy Barry. He used the play and actor for his comic strip's theme and Jiggs.

Eugene O'Neill—Unlike McManus, who was enjoyed by the Irish, playwright Eugene O'Neill was disliked by them. Born of an actor whose parents were "potato famine" Irish and a convent-reared mother, O'Neill wrote feelingly about the despair, heavy drinking, fantasies and failings of the Irish. In *Long Day's Journey Into Night*, he cut through the make-believe lives of his parents, brother and himself to get at the truth of his family.

Other Irish Writers—Other writers born here of Irish Catholic parents are John O'Hara, who wrote *Appointment in Samarra*, Philip Barry who wrote *The Philadelphia Story*, F. Scott Fitzgerald, author of *The*

F. Scott Fitzgerald,
author of *The Great Gatsby*

Great Gatsby and James Thomas Farrell who gave us *Studs Lonigan*, with its fictional South Chicago boy as tragically true-to-life as any character by O'Neill. (Farrell's *Studs* dreams of being a tough guy, and when he does not become a big shot, he loses hope, drinks, lies to himself and dies.) And, then, of course, there was John F. Kennedy, first Irish Catholic President of the United States, who wrote *Profiles in Courage.*

Crafts have been part of the Irish heritage since before the birth of Christ when the first clay pots were fired. The Irish are well known for their hand-blown glassware, their lace making and knitting, their hand-thrown pots and their knubby-textured woven things. But it will be for their words that the Irish will be remembered.

This book cannot help you put words together like the Irishman, George Bernard Shaw. Nor can it set forth rules for a comic strip to be read as eagerly as *Bringing Up Father*. But it can help you to see how a comic strip is constructed once you have created characters who behave in an expected way.

Note below how Nora is serenaded by a group of young men (acceptable behavior). Then, Maggie sings a popular song (considered by Maggie to be acceptable behavior). Now, Jiggs snores (low-brow behavior), and he is bawled out for something he knows is no more objectionable than what has been done by the other two. Note on pages 48 and 49 how this same plot is used by McManus there.

To test your ability as a comic strip artist, select a character (child, cat, puppet, midget, whatever) who is a smart aleck, a tough character, a timid soul, a clown, a bully or whatever. Practice drawing the character and two or three others who will appear with him or her in your strip. In four frames, tell a typical story. Start your story in the first frame, develop it in the second, do a switch in the third, let it backfire on your main character (or help him to achieve something) in the fourth.

The mosaic for the floor of this room in New York's Metropolitan Museum of Art was brought here from Italy. The design was worked out eighteen centuries ago by a Roman artist (or artists) who put thousands of tiny pieces of marble into wet cement one stone at a time. The carpet of stone is a masterpiece.

Italian Mosaics:
Pictures Made with Stones

THE ITALIANS WHO CAME to America by the boatload after the Civil War did not make mosaics. Still, many understood stonework. Some prospered as bricklayers, tile makers, stonemasons, architects, builders and paving contractors.

In Caesar's day, Rome's baths, aqueducts, marble palaces and stone highways were engineering marvels. Later, Italians made great stone carvings. Michelangelo's statues are the best known.

Long ago, many Greeks lived in what is now Italy. Their statues, frescoes (paintings done in wet plaster) and mosaics were later copied by Italians who learned from them. So both the Greeks and the Italians deserve credit for Italy's remarkable carvings, wall paintings and mosaics.

The modern-looking "Bikini Girls" mosaic below was made more than 1500 years ago for a Roman palace on the island of Sicily.

Small flesh-toned stones went into faces in ancient mosaics; larger stones formed background. The problem then, as now, was to place each stone exactly as wanted in wet cement that hardens all too fast.

How to make a mosaic

Materials and Equipment:

Plywood. (Backing for wall plaque shown here is 12″x36″)

Ceramic tiles, ¾″ square. (You will need approximately 300 for a plaque of this size.)

Tile cutter (nippers). (These may be rented from some floor covering stores.) Tile cutters won't be needed if your design is one using only whole tiles.

Sandpaper.

Milk-based glue. (Any glue or cement will do if it does *not* dry too quickly.)

Old table knife or spatula.

Grout (to be mixed with water).

Non-oily solvent. (Lighter fluid or special grout cleaner.)

Planning Stage:

- Before selecting tiles, work out a design. (Decide what colors you want to go where.)

- With the help of your craft store, get ¾″ squares of ceramic tile (loose or with net backing) in the colors you want to make your mosaic.

- Find a place to work in your home or shop where you can keep tiles, backing and other materials in special area until project is completed.

Complete Instructions:

(1) On wrapping paper beside plywood, lay out design with tiles. (2) Glue basic picture to board. Transfer tiles to plywood. With old table knife, "butter" each tile with glue. (Cut tiles to make stems of flowers, and such.) (3) Glue in outside row of tiles. Then, fill in background. (4) Frame plaque with four pieces of molding. Mix grout (water and cement) to the consistency of heavy cream, and pour over tile. (5) Work grout into spaces with hand for 15 minutes; smooth out bubbles, and work away heavy deposits. (6) Wait 30 minutes. Then sponge off surplus. Rinse clean. Let dry 45 minutes and clean off film with lighter fluid. Cover with wet towel for overnight. Shine surface by rubbing. This can be a wall plaque, tray or table top. Sand and stain frame.

Now, for your mosaic:

Draw your design on a paper that you can keep beside you. (To keep each section separate from every other, work out your design with contrasting masses of color.) Now, lay out the design with your tiles as if doing a puzzle. Follow steps below.

1. Plan before glueing.

2. Glue down tiles.

3. Fill in background.

4. Frame, apply grout.

5. Work in grout.

6. Sponge off surplus.

Cabinet making for clocks is a fine art in Iowa's Amana Colonies founded in 1854. The wood is solid cherry or walnut. It is hand carved, finished and rubbed by a craftsman who began learning this work as a child.

Movements for the clocks come from Germany. So did the first Amana colonists who settled briefly in New York State, then moved to Iowa.

Furniture Making in a German Settlement

UNTIL 1932, THE AMANA PEOPLE lived in seven villages on 25,000 acres of rich farmland, in just the way their ancestors had decided to do before leaving Germany. (See picture below taken in early 1900s.) All families in every village belonged to the same branch of the Lutheran church, and all worked for the good of everyone else. These families stayed at night in separate houses, but in the daytime, they cooked in one kitchen, ate in one dining room and did their laundry in one washroom. And they worked in fields, mills and factories that were owned by all.

People from all around came to the Amana colony to buy homemade Amana wine, smoked meats, woolens and furniture. The villages prospered; and finally the people decided to live privately in their own homes like everyone else. So they formed an Amana company and all took shares. They still make homemade things in the villages, but the people keep the money they earn and support their own families.

These doll-sized reproductions of old Amana pieces were made by Harry Zuber, whose picture is on page 4. The light-colored pieces are cherry; the darker pieces, walnut.

How to make a miniature grandfather clock for your dresser or a doll house

Miniature grandfather clock with pocket watch inserted.

(1) On a piece of ¼″ clear pine, cherry or walnut, draw the sections of the clock in the sizes suggested on page 59. (2) Cut parts out of wood with a coping saw. (3) Smooth edges with sandpaper. (4) Build pad for clock's back panel to hold pocket watch, as explained under drawings on page 59. (5) Drill holes and hang pendulum on matchstick, as shown on page 59. (6) Glue side panels and bottom between front and back with Elmer's Glue. Clamp or press until dry. (7) Sand and stain clock with walnut stain. (8) Varnish with clear varnish. (9) Insert pad and attach with two lower screws.

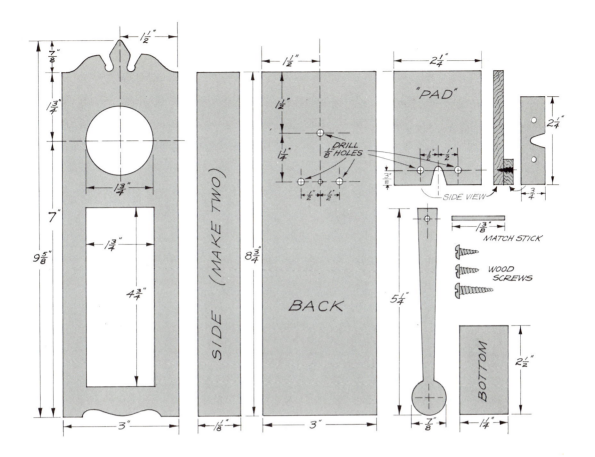

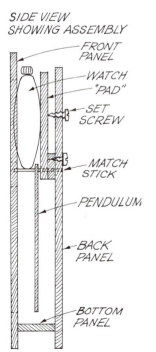

SIDE VIEW
SHOWING ASSEMBLY

FRONT PANEL
WATCH
"PAD"
SET SCREW
MATCH STICK
PENDULUM
BACK PANEL
BOTTOM PANEL

Stain pendulum and interior surfaces of front, back and sides. Assemble as shown at left. When completed clock has been stained and varnished, and is dry, put in pocket watch. (*Simply tighten screw against pad to hold watch in place.*) Later, when watch needs winding, unwind screw, release watch, wind, and return.

Long ago, a Bohemian jeweler cut into glass with a jewelry-making tool. The result was spectacular, and cut glass like this has been popular ever since.

Bohemian artist, Bedrich Egermann, added gold to liquid glass to make ruby glass. Sometimes, he glazed clear glass with a ruby glaze (or fused clear glass with red). Then, etched decorations stood out as the flowers do here.

Glass Decorating
by the Czechs

IN 1848, THE CZECHS OF BOHEMIA were unhappy about being ruled by Austria. To escape, large numbers came to Kansas, Wisconsin and Iowa. They prospered but worried about their European relatives.

In World War I, the Czechs sided against their German neighbors and with the Americans, who sympathized with their plan for an independent government. They suffered, but after the war, they set up their own democratic nation. They lived happily until just before World War II when Germany marched into Czechoslovakia. Finally, the Germans were driven out by the Russians, but the government became Communistic.

Over the years, the Czechs have had a profound effect on glassware. They have found new ways to cut, color, enamel and engrave glass. Their superb creations (like this vase with its engraving of a flood) are in the palaces of kings.

When a castle is etched in red-colored glass which has been plated over colorless glass, the castle stands out.

Deep in Bohemian forests, glassmakers heated sand and quartz to the melting point in big pots over roaring wood fires. Then they poured (or blew) the hot liquid into clay or wooden molds. As the liquid cooled, it hardened in the shape of the mold.

Sometimes the glassmakers added a little gold to the liquid glass. This colored it red. This red glass, called ruby glass, became known as Bohemian glass.

A glass vase or other object taken from the mold was cut, engraved or etched. Or it was enameled, painted or gilded. Or, when the glassblower blew a layer of ruby glass over a layer of white glass in a mold, the ruby glass was engraved to let the clear glass shine through. Or, when colored enamel (which is really a form of glass) was fused to clear glass, a picture was scratched in the enamel. You can do something like this in one of these ways.

Bohemian glass decorators were first to cut into glass with a little

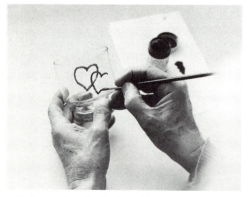

Paint a simple design directly on clean glass with a fine brush, dipped in glass paint.

Or, paint an entire glass with glass paint and let dry. Then, scratch in a design with a jackknife.

Etchings like the one of the Madonna and child on the hand-cut vase have always been popular in Bohemia where most of the people were Roman Catholic.

whirling jeweler's wheel. They also found ways to engrave beautiful pictures in glass with the point of a diamond. And they were first to etch faces, flowers and figures in glass with fluoric acid. Here is a way you can do something with a similar effect on a plastic paperweight:

1. Pour 1½ oz. of Clear Cast Plastic, available at craft shops, in a cup and add catalyst. Stir well. Pour into flexible plastic mold, also available at craft shops. To remove paperweight when hard, turn mold upside down and squeeze plastic. Or buy a plain plastic paperweight also available at craft shops.

2. Scratch face (or piece of fruit or some other simple design) with a sharpened finishing nail or awl in the flat bottom surface of the paperweight.

3. Note how the face is magnified when you look through the rounded surface of the paperweight to the engraving on the back of the flat surface below.

During the annual "Danish Days" in Solvang, California, girls in authentic costumes stir batter with knitting needles to make pancake balls (Aebleskive). Residents, dedicated to preserving their heritage, entertain festival visitors with gymnastics, folk music, dancing and streetside lunches of open-face black bread sandwiches (spread with shrimp and egg, rare roast beef or Danish cheese). But the big attraction is a breakfast of Danish pancake balls. A recipe for Aebleskive is below.

Aebleskive

1 cup flour	*1 cup buttermilk*
1 teaspoon salt	*2 teaspoons sugar*
1 teaspoon soda	*2 eggs separated*
1 teaspoon baking powder	

Put dry ingredients in bowl. Add buttermilk and egg yolks. Fold in beaten egg whites. Heat 2 teaspoons of oil in each of seven depressions in cast iron "monk's pan." Drop in batter and turn ball with knitting needle until round pancake becomes fat and brown, and batter does not stick to needle. Serve with powdered sugar or jam and piping hot coffee. Recipe makes 14 balls.

Scandinavians and
Their Specialities

SWEDEN, DENMARK AND NORWAY have separate governments, but all are called Scandinavians. As fishermen, farmers and lumbermen from the far north, they felt at home in northern Illinois and Indiana, Iowa and Wisconsin when they began to come before the Civil War. Afterward, they also moved into Minnesota and the Dakotas.

Artists in Sweden, which has rich iron ore deposits and great pine forests, make beautiful stainless steel cultery, handsome furniture and "graal glass," which has swirling color burned into it.

Norwegians live near the sea and ship tons of herring, cod, haddock and mackerel to other countries. They enjoy festivals as do the Danes. Denmark's great storytellers include Hans Christian Andersen, and its craftsmen make beautiful hand-decorated pottery and silver products. Denmark's dairy farmers send Danish Blue and other cheeses around the world.

Naturally, Scandinavian festivals feature seafood and cheeses. In Denmark, when the "regesgilde" wreath goes upon a newly framed barn, neighbors come to dance and eat. Then, their tables are loaded with pickled, smoked and baked fish (sometimes, stuffed with sauerkraut), other meats, salads and Danish pastries. These same foods are popular in Swedish communities.

In the old days, Swedish men helped each other put up a barn and mow the fields, and the women helped each other at cheese making time. Their work feasts (and meals at wedding and other celebrations) started off with snacks (smörgasbord), which included among other things hard flat bread (knackebrod), cheeses, herring in a number of forms, pickled beets, meatballs, hard cheese, ham, boiled eggs, potato salad and other good things. Then might come a meal of rolled fish fillets, baked pike, Swedish pot roast or even roast goose, possibly served with red cabbage or creamed vegetables, followed by a dessert of Swedish applecake with vanilla sauce, a berry pudding or a fruit soup.

Recipe for Small Swedish Meatballs

¾ lb. beef, ground	1 tablespoon butter
¼ lb. pork, ground	1½ teaspoons salt
⅓ cup breadcrumbs	¼ teaspoon white pepper
1 cup water and cream	½ teaspoon sugar—optional
1 tablespoon onion, finely chopped	¼ teaspoon nutmeg
To fry: 2–3 tablespoons butter	

Saute onion in butter until golden brown. Soak crumbs in water and cream, then add beef, pork, onion and seasonings, and mix until smooth. Shape into small balls. Fry in butter until evenly browned, shaking the pan to keep balls round. Serve hot or cold.

Holiday Cookies

Two popular Scandinavian cookies at Christmas time are Fattigmands from Norway and Swedish ginger snaps.

Fattigmands (Poor Man's Cake)

3 egg yolks beaten slightly	1 tablespoon melted butter
1 whole egg	¼ teaspoon ground cardamom
4 tablespoons cream	1½ teaspoons brandy or cognac
4 teaspoons sugar	1¼ cups sifted flour

In a large bowl, beat eggs and sugar together thoroughly. Stir in cream, cognac, cardamom and butter. Mix in the flour to make a stiff dough. Cover; chill at least 3 hours.

Heat fat or oil (about 2 inches) to 375°. Divide dough in half. Roll each half very thin, ⅛ to 1/16 inch thick, on well-floured board. Cut dough into 4 x 2-inch diamonds. Make a 1-inch horizontal slit and curl back.

Draw one of the long points of the diamond through the slit; curl back.

Sprinkle Fattigmands with confectioners' sugar.

Fry in hot fat about 15 seconds on each side or until light brown. Drain. Before serving, sprinkle with confectioners' sugar.

Swedish Ginger Snaps (Pepparkakor)

⅔ cup brown sugar

⅔ cup dark corn syrup

1 teaspoon ginger

1 teaspoon cinnamon

½ teaspoon cloves

¾ tablespoon baking soda

⅔ cup butter

1 egg

5 cups sifted flour

Heat sugar, syrup and spices to boiling point. Add baking soda and pour mixture over butter in a bowl. Stir until butter melts. Add egg and flour and blend thoroughly. Form into a ball and chill. Roll out dough to ⅛ inch thick on floured board and cut with fancy cutters. Place on greased baking sheet and bake in 325° F. oven for 8–10 minutes. When cool, decorate if you like with icing made from ½ cup confectioner's sugar and ½ an egg white beaten together until smooth. Force icing through a fine paper tube.

Symbols on decorated Ukrainian Easter eggs, known as pysanky, have religious meanings. The eight-pointed star, once the sign of the sun god, symbolizes Christ. The cross signifies suffering, death and Resurrection, and wheat promises fertility and a bountiful harvest. Unbroken lines that encircle all Ukrainian eggs foretell everlasting life.

Ukrainian Easter Eggs

O N EASTER SUNDAY, WHEREVER UKRAINIANS celebrate, decorated eggs that look like jewels are passed from friend to friend. These eggs are not eaten. They are displayed in the home and are believed by many to have the power to prevent fires and other disasters.

The decorating of the eggs is done with a *kistka*, which is a writing tool, dipped in melted beeswax. And the eggs, which go through several dye baths and come out brilliantly colored, are known as *pysanky* (from the verb *pysaty*, which means *to write*). The method by which the eggs go from white to lovely creations with colorful symbols is similar to the wax resist (batik) method of dyeing fabrics.

For centuries in Ukraine, an eastern European country on the Black Sea, about the size of Texas, Christians took eggs they had decorated to their church the night before Easter to have them blessed by the priest. Then, the next morning, they gave their elegant eggs to friends whom they joined for a breakfast of home-baked bread (paska), spicy home-ground sausage, roast ham, beet and horseradish relish, cheese and boiled eggs, dyed for this occasion in a solid color. Both the cooked eggs (krashanky) and the decorated ones (pysanky) reminded all that in the springtime life begins again.

Life has begun again in America for thousands of Ukrainians whose fertile homeland has been overrun by powerful enemies at various times and whose country is now controlled by Russia. In New York

City, where there are 100,000 Ukrainians, and in Connecticut, Pennsylvania, New Jersey, the Minneapolis–St. Paul area of Minnesota and in other communities where many Ukrainians have settled, the ancient folk art of egg decorating becomes more popular every year.

In Hartford, eighty-year-old Nicholas Mulicky, a husky ironworker who was taught to decorate eggs by his mother in Ukraine, told us that the women in his family always began the egg decorating process with the sign of the cross—"God help me." Their prayer was that their beautiful eggs would protect their loved ones from harm. He said that in Ukraine each region has its own symbols and favorite colors. In the western section, from which he came, geometric designs are popular; in the east, flowers are favored. However, in America, he decorates eggs with whatever design suits his fancy.

A favorite of children as well as of artists who are learning the craft, he talks to groups at clubs, schools and other meetings places. His audience learns that most decorators work out their egg designs in white, yellow, orange, red and black; and that dyes in Ukraine, when he was growing up, were made from saffron, flowers, onion peels, berries and walnut stain. He says that a girl who gives a boy a decorated egg on Easter is offering her love, which she knows is accepted if the boy does not return her egg.

Some decorators remove the insides of the egg through a small hole. Mr. Mulicky does not. He knows that eventually the yolk and white inside the shell will dry up.

For pysanky, you will need fresh white eggs; scouring powder; pencil; kistka; beeswax; candle; 3-pint glass jars; dish towel; long-handled slotted spoon; yellow, orange, red and black food colorings; tissue; small paintbrush; varnish.

Select smooth, white fresh eggs with no oily deposits inside. (Hold up to light. Do you see bubbles, lines, dots showing through the shell? Such eggs will break after decorating.) Do not boil eggs. Wash with scouring powder. Rinse in cool water and pat dry.

To decorate:
(1) Plan your design on paper. Then, sketch lightly on egg with pencil.
(2) Heat kistka filled with wax over candle. (3) Cover egg by drawing with kistka where you want design to show white. (The white eggshell

will not be revealed until you melt off wax.) (4) Dip egg in yellow dye. Remove, pat dry with tissue. Now wax with kistka the areas where you want the decorated egg to be yellow. Then, dip egg in orange dye. (Or skip this step and go to red.) Now, draw on your egg with kistka where you want egg to stay orange (or red, if you have dipped in red dye). Remove. Pat dry. Continue covering areas with wax until you have all the colors you want. Make sure you begin with the lightest color and finish with the darkest one. Finally, dip egg (which may look red but has white, yellow and orange markings protected by wax) in black dye. This is your final color. All of your egg not covered with wax will now be black. Pat egg dry. (5) To remove wax, warm your egg over a candle and let wax melt away. (Or for faster results, warm one or more of your waxed eggs in oven.) When wax melts away, you will see all the colors—white, yellow, orange and red designs—on a black egg. (6) Polish with tissue. Finally, put a coat of clear varnish on your egg with a small paintbrush to preserve colors and design.

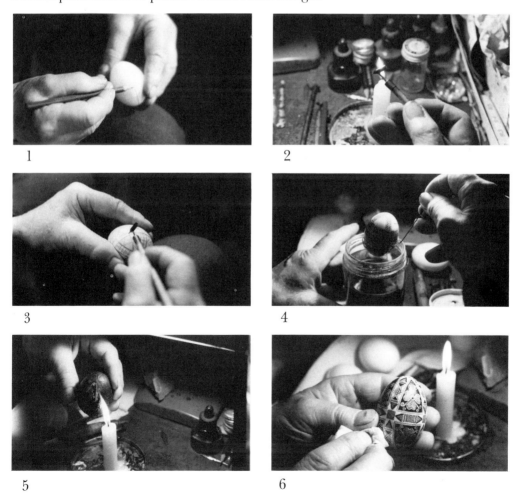

1

2

3

4

5

6

Yodelers in New Glarus, Wisconsin, wear traditional embroidered Swiss waist-coats when they sing twice a week at Robbie's Yodel Club.

From the Land of William Tell,
Swiss Embroideries

O N LABOR DAY WEEKEND, at New Glarus, Wisconsin (settled by Swiss), an outdoor drama tells the story of William Tell, who supposedly was sentenced to die in 1307 for resisting an Austrian officer. He was freed when he shot an apple from his son's head, but was thrown into chains when he said that he would have killed the officer had his arrow killed his son. On the way by boat to prison, Tell was released during a storm to save the boat. This time, he killed the officer and later led Switzerland's revolt against Austria, which brought independence.

At various times in history, some Swiss people came to America. One group settled in 1710 in New Bern, North Carolina, which became the state's first capital. The New Glarus group came in 1845, a year of riots in Switzerland. Today, their tidy, peaceful town is surrounded by dairy farms like the ones their ancestors had in Europe. In their local

The people of New Glarus, Wisconsin, stage an outdoor drama each year that tells the story of William Tell, a Swiss national hero.

Swiss boys wear bells like those on horses when they pull toboggans in annual parade. Note embroidery on jacket.

shops, Swiss Americans sell Wisconsin cheese and yogurt, Swiss chocolates and pastries, and embroideries made by Upright Swiss Embroideries, whose New Glarus proprietor was born in Switzerland. And once a year they put on a pageant, which attracts thousands.

Switzerland, like America, was settled by people from many nations. Four languages are spoken there—German, Italian, French and Romansh (a language derived from spoken Latin). The country has magnificent mountains, which bring enthusiastic tourists who climb, ski, enjoy the scenery and attend regional celebrations. Shops sell cheese, clocks, watches and embroideries.

Some Swiss things are embroidered by hand, but most of the embroidery today is done in factories by complicated embroidery machines powered by energy produced by swift-running mountain streams. Similar machines can be seen in the embroidery factory in New Glarus, Wisconsin.

When you sew two pieces of material together or hem up a skirt or sew up a tear, you try to make tiny stitches that do not show. But when you do embroidery, you want your stitches to show. Your stitches

Embroidery in first picture was made on machine with 1,024 needles; lace in second picture was made by a sophisticated machine in 8½ hours; embroidered fabrics like those in third picture are made by hand and in factories.

In Colonial times, the art of embroidery was passed down from mother to daughter. Many homes had "paintings" done with a needle. These "peacock pillowcases" are in the Tolliver house at Big Stone Gap, Virginia.

become the embroidered design.

When you embroider, whether you are putting your initials on a handkerchief or embroidering a flower on a table mat or "painting a picture" with threads of many colors for a wall hanging, what you want to show are the stitches on the top of your material. As an embroiderer, your only tools will be a needle, threads, scissors, material on which to embroider and, perhaps, a hoop or frame to hold that material taut. You can trace or make a free-hand drawing on the material (or buy a printed design on material to be embroidered or a printed transfer pattern). Then you can begin to sew with whatever stitch seems best for your design.

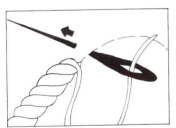

1. Outline stitch

2. Back stitch

3. Chain stitch

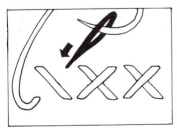

4. Cross stitch

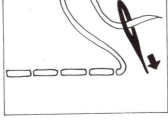

5. Running stitch

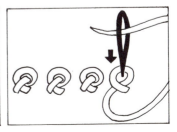

6. French knot

The glistening fort with the flags went up nearly a century ago at Quebec's annual ice carnival in Montreal. The eleven-story reproduction of Camelot, below, made of 11,000 blocks of ice, was a major attraction in 1886 at the first big U.S. winter carnival at St. Paul, Minnesota. Now, many towns and cities have snow and ice festivals.

Inspired by Canadians:
Building of Ice
and Sculptures of Snow

ANADA IS LARGER than the United States but has fewer people; much of its land in the far north is too cold for farming and too inaccessible in winter for industry. Nevertheless, Canada is a rich country of farmers, fishermen, hunters, lumbermen, miners and manufacturers, more than half of whom have ancestors who came from England, Scotland, Ireland and Wales. (Many of the others came from France and settled in Quebec; still others came from Russia, Norway, Sweden, Holland, Italy and Poland. And, of course, there were Indians in Canada when the white men arrived.) Two languages are spoken— English and French. Most of those who speak English go to a Protestant church, while the others, who are French Canadian, go to the Catholic church.

Because almost all of Canada has long, cold winters, the people have learned to use and enjoy cold weather. Winter sports and winter carnivals are an important part of Canadian life.

FIGURE WITHOUT ARMATURE   FIGURE WITH ARMATURE

How to make a statue of snow (with and without an inner frame or armature) and an igloo

1. *Figure without armature*
    - Do not make a snow statue taller than six feet without an armature.
    - Give your statue a broad base of packed snow. (Make a dog that is sitting rather than standing on four thin legs.)
    - Dress a queen in a long robe or make a man whose two legs are close together (which are a pillar of snow).
    - Make a drawing of your sitting dog, man, queen or other figure before you begin.
    - Collect more snow in a pile than you will need so that you can pack solidly as you build. (Powdery snow won't pack well. Wet snow with water to make workable slush.)
    - Build your figure handful by handful, packing mushy snow down solidly.
    - Put a large block or ball of hard-packed snow on your figure for its head. With a knife or long-handled spoon, dig away for eyes, mouth, nostrils. Build out for forehead, cheeks, nose and ears.

2. *Figure with armature*
    - Draw a picture of the statue you want to make. Build a simple frame out of sturdy boards. (With this frame for the snow to adhere to, you can make a running man, a dancing girl, a stork on one leg or another figure in motion.)

IGLOO   FRAME FOR SNOW BLOCK HOUSE   BLOCK CARVING

3. *Igloo*
   - Eskimos make building blocks out of packed snow, which they set in a circle, cutting each block to lean in a little. They put row on row, slanting blocks in, until the house has a round dome. Finally, they put one block at the top center. As the blocks freeze together, the Eskimos fill in with mushy snow, which soon freezes. The entrance is through a low tunnel that slants up, to keep the warm air in.
   - In northern Canada and Alaska, this kind of house stays solid all winter, but farther south, the blocks may melt and fall in. To prevent this, you can build a house over a wire frame. Put a large center pole in the ground as for a tent and stake out four poles to hold up the outer walls. Then, build a wire mesh frame over and around the poles. Pack the frame with mushy snow, spray with water to freeze. Draw lines to look like separations between blocks.

How to carve ice

You cannot build up or "mend" a figure made out of ice as you can one made with snow. So, chip ice away carefully as if carving stone. (When using artificial ice, which is especially brittle, chip away little by little.)

Materials needed: ruler, T-square, small hammer, small chisel, saw and a block of ice.

Before carving (a centerpiece for your Christmas dinner, perhaps) make a full-scale drawing of your proposed dancer, squirrel, Christmas tree, turkey, pumpkin, cornucopia, fish or whatever. (You may want to make a small-scale model of your intended carving in soap.)

With your ruler and T-square, square off your ice block and saw off jagged edges.

Lightly scratch in the outline of your figure with the sharp end of your chisel.

Work from the top down, tapping your chisel against the ice to chip away a little ice at a time. Work gently because as ice melts it becomes more fragile.

Allow for as large a base as possible to support your ice carving. Keep figure in freezer or protected place outdoors until time to display.

Eskimo art was small because the walrus tooth carried and carved by a hunter was small. Sometimes, a picture was engraved in ivory (as in engraving) and sometimes figures were carved out of ivory (as in the dog sled carving) but the carving always told a real story.

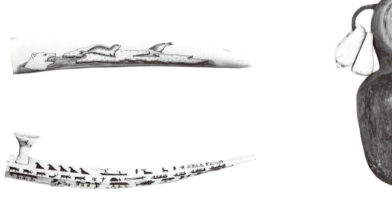

Some Eskimo carvings, like the engraving of the seals and bear on the ice floe, are purely decorative. Other Eskimo art objects were useful. The ivory pipe records birds and animals actually sighted in a hunt. And the carved wooden face is really a float for a fishing net.

Art by Eskimos

THE WORLD'S 40,000 ESKIMOS who live in northern Canada, Alaska, the Aleutian Islands, Greenland and Siberia are descended from a people who have battled the cold for centuries just to stay alive. Until recently, most of them wore furs from animals they killed with a bow and arrow or a rifle and ate the meat of these animals and fish. (The very word, *Eskimo*, means "eater of meat.") The pictures they engraved in ivory, like the one below, explain how they hunted land animals with rifles and sea mammals with harpoons.

Eskimos and American Indians were here long before the white men. Most people believe they crossed over the Bering Strait from Siberia thousands of years ago.

You can get a feeling of how an Eskimo made an engraving by carving with a finishing nail on a white plastic bottle that has held dishwashing liquid. Make a simple drawing, maybe one that illustrates something you have done or seen recently. Rub carbon, which you can collect by holding a rock above a candle, into your cut marks. Then, clean away smudges with a damp cloth. You will have a reasonable facsimile of an engraving done by an Eskimo.

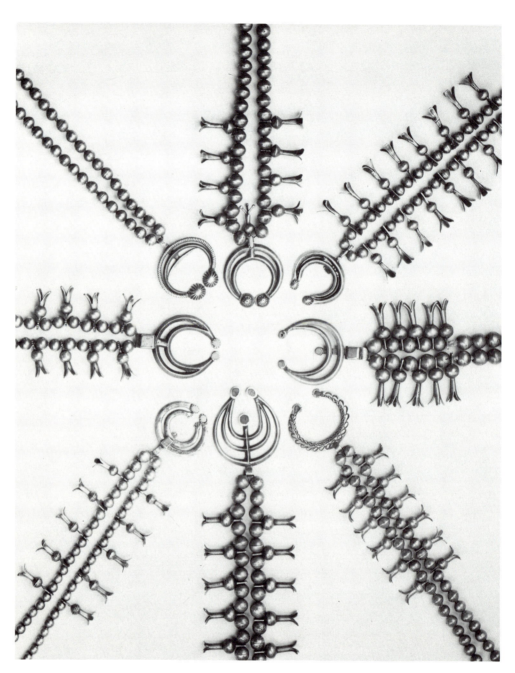

These old silver necklaces are made with heavy round beads and petallike pieces of silver that curve up and out like flowers. Such "squash blossom" designs probably were adapted by the Indians from "pomegranate" designs made by Spanish silversmiths in Mexico. The crescent or "naja" in the center goes back to the Moors, who invaded and conquered Spain long before Columbus discovered America.

Jewelry by Indians
in the Great Southwest

THE NAVAJOS, ZUNIS AND HOPIS were taught to work silver by the Spanish. But way back in prehistoric times, they were making beads, nose rings, necklaces and earrings out of bones, feathers, turquoises, pipestone, coal, molded clay and shells. And the designs of many of their silver things have their roots in ornaments made long ago.

About 1850, a few Navajos began working with iron as smiths had done in Mexico. By 1870, they were making silver bracelets and conchos for belts by hammering silver dollars and pesos into disks, into which they could stamp a design. By 1900, they were making silver jewelry in huge quantities, which they sold through traders to tourists. Today, silverwork in many tribes is an art.

The Navajos cast molten silver in molds for beads and pins. They also cut wrist bands, pendants and conchos for belts.

Indian bola ties were inspired by the South American bola weapon, which has heavy balls tied to the ends of a strong cord. (It is thrown by a cowboy to entangle the legs of a cow.) As American cowboys made bola ties popular, Indian jewelry makers converted medallions and antique pins into bolas. Today, bola ties for both men and women are sold by the thousands in the Southwest.

Cut into the top layer of this bracelet, made by Hopi silverworker Lawrence "Little Bear" Saufkie, is an Indian pottery design. The lower piece has been chemically darkened. After soldering, the dark lower piece sets off the design.

The Zunis, who learned silversmithing from the Navajos, implant turquoises in silver. (Sometimes, they cut the blue-green stones to look like kachina dolls, roadrunners or cactus plants.) And the Hopis, who learned from the Zunis, are masters of overlay. They cut a design in silver and lay this over a second chemically darkened layer of silver so that the under sheet shows through in places.

How to make a bola tie

Select an attractive shell, sand dollar, antique button or pin or a tumble-polished rock. With epoxy glue, fasten a bola tieback (which you can buy in a craft store or order from *Beads and More*, 4234 Craftsman Court, Scottsdale, Arizona, 85251) to the back of your shell, button or rock. Tie a 44″ shoestring or leather bola tie cord (which you also can get from *Beads and More*) through the bola tieback. Wear your bola tie instead of a more conventional tie or scarf.

How to make Indian Jewelry

Under the direction of Alberta Pfeiffer of Hadlyme, Connecticut, children working in summer library classes made simple ornaments—with 18-gauge "Nugold" wire and a long-nosed pliers—adapted from Indian designs.

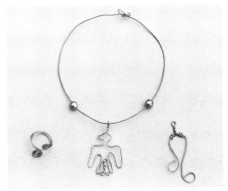

Inspired by an 18-inch bird claw, beautifully carved from a single sheet of mica, which had been buried for 2,000 years in an Ohio mound, silversmith Peter Kunkel of Woodbury, Connecticut, made the superb silver necklace below without squash blossoms but with a squash blossom feeling. Like a pioneer smith, he cut and shaped two halves of every bead by hand and, then, with a jeweler's saw, cut the claws for his necklace one by one out of sheet silver. He set blue stones (hand cut from a slab of Persian turquoise) into the silver pieces for a stunning effect.

(1) Hand of Peter Kunkel as he pounds bead.

(2) Hands cutting with jeweler's saw.

(3) Peter Kunkel's necklace.

In Java, where batiks with glorious color have been painted by hand for more than a thousand years, these young women took two months to prepare the fabric and wax and dye this batik. Note how the artists have worked a mythical eagle into their design. The bird is reserved for the robes of a few East Indian sultans.

Batiks from Java

To make a batik, the artist paints a picture on white, treated cotton with melted wax. Then, she or he dips the waxed material into cold water that contains dye. (This darkens the background but not the picture under the wax.) When the artist boils out the wax, the picture shows up white on a dark background. Other colors can be added in the same way.

Long ago, in Java, "fabric painting" was done by the daughters of noble families, who had their own batiks as the Scots had tartans. In the 1600s, Dutch traders took batiks from Java to Holland where fabric makers tried "resist dyeing" without great artistic success. (Later, American designers tried batik making but could not match the richness of Javanese fabrics.) Recently, courses in batik making have been given by experts in American schools, and artists here are creating batiks that have originality and charm.

In Java, batik makers wash and dry their cotton cloth and then soak it in coconut oil. Then, they boil it, dry it in the sun, pound it and soak it again in rice water. Finally, they hang it over a frame and

A Javanese girl waxes fabric between each color bath. Reddish brown and blue design (center) took only a few waxings and dye dips. Flowers and butterflies (right) called for six months of fabric treatment.

"paint" both sides with a *tjanting* applicator that spouts hot wax. They dye the cotton with a dark color like indigo, boil out the wax, dry the cotton, restarch and then rewax for dyeing with a lighter color. Their finished batik may take months.

Simple Way to Make a Batik

EQUIPMENT:
Picture frame or stretcher
Push pins
Stove (or hot plate with temperature control)
Double boiler
Rubber gloves
Plastic bucket or large plastic bowl for dip-dyeing
Large pan for boiling wax out of fabric
Electric iron

MATERIALS:
Cotton or muslin sheeting cut to right size for wall hanging, scarf or pillow cover
Charcoal pencil
Artist's brushes in three sizes (plus tjanting pen, if wanted)
Melted white candles or paraffin wax
Two permanent household dyes, red and dark blue
Newspapers
Detergent
Paper toweling

(1.) Draw design or simple picture of flower on sheeting with soft pencil. Stretch sheeting over picture frame and secure with push pins. Heat wax to melting point (but not smoking point) in double boiler. (2.) Go over lines on fabric with fine brush dipped in this melted wax or with *tjanting* pen filled with melted wax. In your finished batik, these lines will be white. (3.) Now, with artist's brush, paint wax over all areas of sheeting that you want to remain white. When wax on material is dry, "ball up" material to break the hardened wax. This will allow color to touch the fabric when material is dipped in dye, creating "crackle" or veins of red and purple color. Dissolve red dye in hot water and let cool. (4.) Soak waxed fabric in cool red water for 60 minutes. Remove and dry by laying wet fabric on folded newspapers and blotting with more newspapers placed on top. Gently rub hands over top newspapers to blot up excess dye in fabric underneath. Now hang up moist fabric to drip dry; if fabric is not completely dry, wax

1

2

3

4

5

6

will not penetrate. Apply more wax, covering all areas where you want clear red color. Dissolve blue dye in hot water and let cool. Then, soak your waxed fabric for 60 minutes in cool blue water. The blue over the unwaxed red color will give a purplish color. (5.) When fabric is dry, remove wax by ironing fabric between two paddings of absorbent paper toweling. To remove final traces of wax, boil fabric in water containing detergent. Rinse in clear water. Iron dry. (6.) Your batik will have a handsome design in red, white and purple.

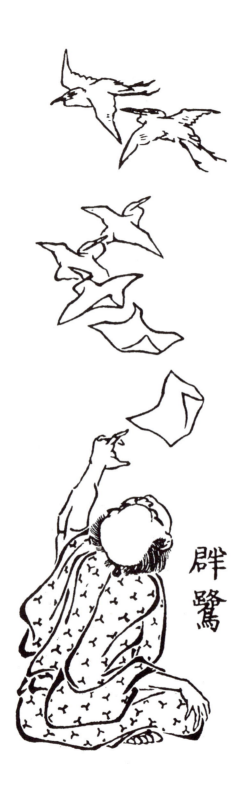

群鷺

In 1850, this Japanese
print illustrated the story
of a magician who folded a
paper crane that fluttered
its wings and flew away.

By the Japanese
Origami (Paper Folding)

ORIGAMI IS POPULAR in San Francisco, where there are many Japanese Americans, a Japanese Cultural Center and a Japanese Tea Garden in Golden Gate Park. And it is taught at the Origami Center in New York and in colleges and museums across the country.

In the past, we prevented people from Japan from coming to the United States to live. We entered World War II when Japan bombed the American fleet in Hawaii and ended it four years later by dropping two atom bombs on Japan. Now, we have helped Japan to become a strong industrial nation, and we import many Japanese products. Japanese students come to our universities and American students go there to study Japanese movie-making, architecture, gardening and art, which includes origami.

Long ago Japanese art was influenced by Chinese art. Japan, on tiny islands off the coast of Asia, contains no more land than California and

for centuries was a country of fishermen. China, on Asia's mainland, is larger than any other country except the Soviet Union and was producing magnificent art four thousand years ago. But over the years the Japanese have done more than copy. Their music, plays, paintings and origami reveal that the Japanese are gifted and original.

How to Make a Silver Star out of Foil

Lay a piece of foil 12″ x 15″ in front of you the long way. (Or for a smaller star, use a piece, 8″ x 10″.)

Fold the foil in half as shown.
Fold the lower right-hand corner over to the halfway mark as shown.
Fold the right edge down to the left crease as shown.
Fold the lower crease up to right edge as shown.
Cut straight through paper where line is marked "cut." *
Unfold paper, being careful not to tear foil.

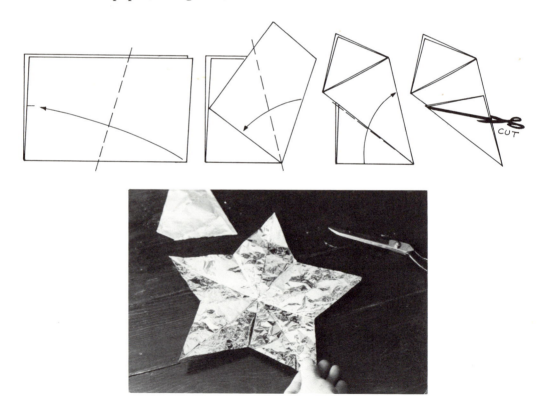

* *Pure origami does not require cutting or pasting, but for the beginner we recommend the star with one cut.*

How to make the male duck at the right
on the pond at the bottom of this page

Note: Fold forward on a dotted line. Fold backward on a dot-dash line.

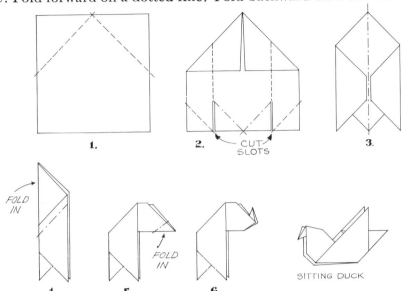

(1) Begin with a 6-inch square of paper, folding upper two corners forward as shown. (2) Cut slits in crease at the bottom as shown. (3) Fold backward on dot-dash line to make tail; now fold forward in four places as shown. (4) Crease in center on dot-dash line. (5) Fold in for neck (see photograph). (6) Spread head, fold in for beak. Spread lower edges to make sitting duck.

This hollow horse was put into the tomb of a Chinese nobleman more than 1200 years ago. It is made of baked clay and is a little more than a foot high and is a foot-and-a-half long. Like other pottery horses made during the T'ang Dynasty (a period of rule by a powerful Chinese family), it has a cream-colored glaze and is streaked with brown, amber and blue.

From the Chinese: Pottery Figures

CHINA IS A HUGE COMMUNIST COUNTRY in eastern Asia with a population four times as large as that of the United States. For centuries it was ruled by emperors, one of whom built a great wall along the country's northern border in 228 B.C. to keep foreigners away. The Chinese invented gunpowder 2,000 years ago and were printing from wooden blocks long before others. Centuries ago, they painted landscapes and portraits, made beautiful statues and built pagodas that were nine stories high.

From the 1850s to the '80s, many Chinese laborers came to work in California. Because they were different from other Americans, they were abused, and eventually laws limited the number of incoming workers. (Only Chinese teachers, students, merchants, diplomats and Chinese wives of Americans were welcome.) Now, America appreciates more fully the art of China and the contributions of Chinese immigrants.

In China, ancient bronze statues guard old palaces. Stone lions and dragons guard ancient cave temples. Figures of Buddha welcome visi-

A thousand years ago, hand-painted musicians were put in a T'ang tomb to entertain a dead nobleman.

Winged lions, dragons and animals like these have been found in China's early cave temples, religious grottoes and tombs.

tors to religious grottoes.

Many American museums have Chinese figures taken from tombs. One may have clay servants or musicians that were buried with a nobleman. Another may have an earthenware camel (signifying that the dead man was a merchant trader) or a glazed pottery hound (a dead man's pet) or a clay horse (saddled for its master). Some of the figures have been shaped in a clay mold. Others were molded by hand and then fired and glazed.

Most of the clay figures in stores in the Chinatowns of San Francisco, New York and other large cities are not ancient. They are new figures made to look like old ones.

Easy Ways to Make a Figure without Firing

Use Sculptamold, which you can find at a craft store. When you mix the powder with water it changes to a claylike material. The clay stays workable for 30 minutes before it sets like plaster of Paris.

To make a plaque, press the material into a mold. To make a mold yourself, place some sand in a container and wet it. Then model the shape you want in the sand, remembering that your plaque will be the opposite of your mold. When your mold is ready, make your clay and pat it into the mold. When the clay is dry, it will free itself from the drying sand. Before the plaque dries completely, put a cord in the back so that you can hang it up.

To make a three dimensional head, make *two* molds (for the front of the head and the back of the head) by pressing two sides of a three dimensional head into wet sand. Fill both molds with the claylike material and just before the head is dry, press the two sides together, then let dry completely.

To make a figure like the horse, opposite, do your modeling over a foil armature.

How to Make a Horse with Sculptamold
(which you can buy at a crafts store)

- Make an armature out of twisted foil that will give support but will not interfere with shape of your horse.
- Place your armature on newspaper so that your horse will not stick to your table.
- Work on lazy Susan on a small table if possible. Or work in a room where you have space to move around the table as you work.
- Work at eye level, either by sitting to work or by placing a small table on a larger one at eye level, if you stand.
- Keep in mind that the Sculptamold you are working with will set up in 30 minutes. Mix only a little at a time, just enough for a half-hour's use. Go back later and add wet Sculptamold to the horse you have begun.
- Keep hands clean when working. (Wash under hose or in bucket rather than in sink where you may clog drain.)
- "Cure" your finished horse by drying in sun or in oven at 200°.
- To give your horse a smooth surface, rub horse with coarse sand paper.
- Paint your horse with acrylic paint, if you prefer a color to white.

An artist at the Cellulose Corporation built up this horse gradually with Sculptamold over a foil armature. You can follow his pattern or model a figure of your own. Whatever you do, draw your figure on paper before you mix your first batch of Sculptamold.

Shoemakers in all Moroccan villages make elaborately decorated shoes. They work with leather made from the skins of goats and kids, which is unusually soft and workable. Other makers of shoes (and gloves and bags) like to work with this soft leather, so goat and kid skins from Morocco are shipped around the world.

Leatherwork
from Morocco

THERE ARE MORE GOATS and sheep in Morocco than there are people. Their soft skins are admired everywhere, and shiploads go out regularly from this North African kingdom. Before shipping, the skins are treated (tanned), which changes the skins to leather.

One soft, pebbled leather, made from goatskin and tanned in a brew made from the bark of sumac trees, is produced in many countries, but is called "Morocco leather" because it was first produced there. But many other varieties of leather are produced in Morocco, too. Some leather stays in Morocco and is changed there to harnesses, water and food containers, sandals, tents and drums.

Leather workers carve leather made from thick cowhide or sheepskin as we carve wood. They incise (engrave) decorations in their sandals made from goatskin and in their saddles. And they dye pieces of leather to make charms, which they wear around their necks. Sometimes for fans, pouches or shoes, they may combine several leatherworking techniques, first dying leather a dark red, then incising a pattern in the leather and rubbing white chalk into the grooves. Finally they may even applique pieces of leather (dyed in light colors) on the dark material.

How to Make a Key Fob,
Barrette and Wristband out of Leather

To trace any of the patterns, opposite, on leather, you will need cardboard, a sharp pencil, sharp shears and a scrap of leather.* And for the key fob and barrette, you will need a rotary punch to make holes.

Trace your pattern for fob, barrette or band on cardboard. Cut out pattern with sharp scissors, making sure not to fuzz edges. Then, lay cardboard pattern on leather, tracing outline on leather with sharp pencil. Cut out leather for fob, barrette or band with shears. Punch holes for rivet in key fob with rotary punch, Do the same for dowel for barrette, placing holes closer together if you plan to wear on small section of hair.

Leather-working tools and supplies needed for one or all of these projects:

- *Cardboard*
- *Pencil*
- *Heavy scissors (and punch if you make key fob)*
- *Scraps of leather*
- *Rotary punch*
- *Used ball point pen with no ink*
- *Rawhide mallet*
- *Tempered masonite*
- *Sponge*
- *Stamping tools (plus swivel knife if you are going to carve as well as stamp)*

- *Bevel*
- *Brown penetrating dye*
- *Rags*
- *Paints and small brush, if you want colors*
- *Wax (or natural shoe polish)*
- *Soft cloth*
- *Newspapers (and, perhaps, rubber gloves) to protect work table (and hands) from dye stains*

In the beginning, buy scraps of economy grade cowhide leather (preferably 7–8 oz. weight) from a leathercrafter in your town. Later, if you go on to make wallets, bags, lamps, boxes and other large items, you can buy a side or back hide. And for special projects, you can buy suede or pigskin or goat, deer, antelope or a more exotic skin, depending on your project.

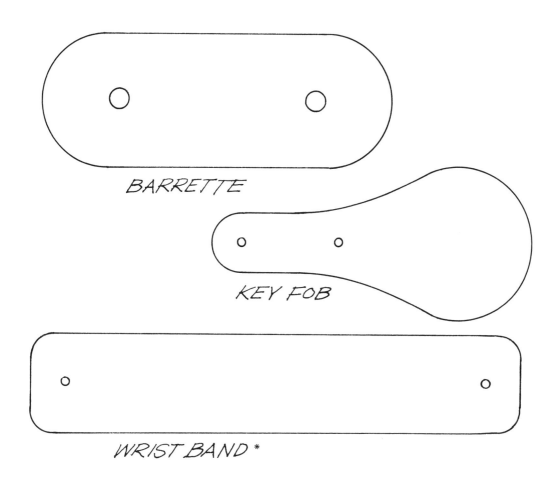

BARRETTE

KEY FOB

WRIST BAND *

Enlarge to fit a larger wrist.

To Make Your Key Fob

In addition to the tools and supplies listed on page 100, you will need one key ring, one medium rivet and a rivet setter.

Stamp design into smooth side of leather, as explained in stamping instructions for all leatherwork on page 103.

Apply brown penetrating dye to both sides of leather with rag (and daub along cut edge with dauber) and let dry overnight. Next morning, if you want color in your design, paint with small brush dipped in acrylic paint and let dry another day. Wax with natural shoe polish and buff with soft cloth.

1. Cut out leather

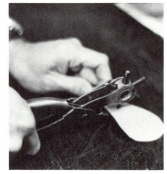

2. Punch holes

3. Bevel edges

4. Wet leather

5. Stamp leather

6. Cut design

7. Dye edges

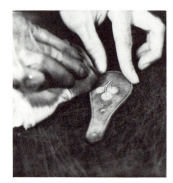

8. Dye leather

9. Rivet

Simplified directions for making key fob, barrette and band were supplied by Sam Boazman, leathercraftsman from New Fairfield, Connecticut, who posed for all "how to" photographs.

Put small end of fob through ring and align rivet holes (which have been punched as shown in pattern with rotary punch). Put rivet post in holes, placing concave rivet setter on cap and tap sharply with mallet to set rivet tightly in leather (so that it does not turn).

To Make your Barrette

Stamp as suggested for fob and dye both leather and 6-inch wooden dowel (which you have sharpened in pencil sharpener) with dark brown dye. Dry leather overnight and buff.

To Make your Wristband

Stamp, dye, paint and buff as for fob and barrette, but carve your name rather than flowers into band if you want. Draw letters on leather and go to work with a swivel knife. Cut one-third of way through leather with knife held in slanting position toward you allowing knife to swivel as you follow curved lines.

Leather barrette   Leather wristband

How to stamp leather with embossing tool

Or with metal button, square nut, bolt head, old table fork, raised design on old spoon or some other metal object. See what interesting things you can find to use for stamping a pattern.

Trace design with pencil on dry leather which you will emboss. Dip leather in water for about 2 minutes. When surface dries, place on masonite board. Put embossing tool or other metal object on leather as marked and tap with hammer or mallet. Do this in place after place until design is finished.

At Christmastime in Mexico, blind-folded children try to knock down a piñata which is suspended from the ceiling. If they strike the piñata (which is clay or papier-maché or a combination of both) hard and firmly, it will break. Then candy and toys spill out on the floor.

For Holiday Cheer . . .
Mexico's Piñata

SOUTH OF THE RIO GRANDE RIVER, which runs along our southern border, is Mexico. This friendly country is peopled with pure-blooded Indians, descendants of Indians who married Spaniards, and pure-blooded Spaniards and other Europeans with no Indian blood. (This last group includes emigrants from the United States, Canada and Europe.) All members of the three groups who were born or naturalized in Mexico are Mexicans.

The Mexican language is Spanish mixed with Indian, and the church for most of the people is Roman Catholic. The people love *fiestas*, and they have many celebrations based on their religious beliefs. By far the most important is their Christmas celebration that lasts from December 16th to Christmas Eve.

At a Christmas party, villagers re-enact the search for shelter of Mary and Joseph in Bethlehem. They sing in the streets and knock on many doors but are turned away. Finally, they reach the house of their host and are welcomed to an evening of dancing and eating. The climax comes with the breaking of the piñata, which is a bright-colored object made of clay and papier-maché.

Usually, the piñata is shaped like a star or a bell or a stork. It hangs from a ceiling beam and has a clay pot for a belly. The pot is filled with candy, nuts and gifts. When the pot is broken with a stick by a blindfolded child, the good things fall out.

Many Americans hang a piñata in their home on Christmas Eve or at birthday parties or other festivities. Like Mexicans, they tie a rope to the rope that holds the piñata, and then one by one blindfolded people, generally children, try to strike it with a stick and break it. At last someone does, the clay pot breaks and down come the gifts.

From the time of Julius Caesar

Some say that the *pignata* (as first called) was an old Roman game. At the end of harvesting, workers hung a clay pot, filled with nuts and fruits, from the branch of a tree and let blindfolded players try to break the pot with a stick. The custom spread with the armies of Julius Caesar to Spain, where the Iberians decorated *piñata* pots in bright colors for their harvest festivals. Later, the Spaniards introduced the piñata to Mexico, and there the clay pot at fiesta time became a joyful work of art.

At first, Mexicans simply wound their pots with colored strips of paper. But soon the more ambitious artists began making bulls they had seen at bullfights out of papier-maché which they built out from their pots. Today, many artists make a "skeleton" of wire around a pot and cover it with papier-maché.

Anyone can make a piñata

To make a simple star, follow these three steps. (1) Build a frame of wood with a large enough belly or center hole to hold a good-sized pot. (2) For your pot, use a clay flowerpot, an old glass baking dish or a breakable mixing bowl. Or make a papier-maché pot by covering a fish bowl with paste-covered strips of newspaper and drying it overnight. In the morning, cut away the two halves of the paper covering with a razor blade and lay more paste-covered strips over the two halves to hold them together. Anchor your pot in the wooden frame. (3) Build points for your star with rolled-up newspapers. Wind bright-colored crepe paper around frame to fill out star.

Hang clothesline-high for a party. Give a stick to one blindfolded child after another until someone breaks the pot.

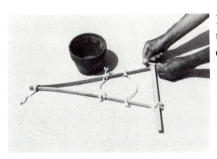

Make a triangular frame of light wood strips that will fit around pot. Put rope anchor in center to contain it.

Tie three strings to frame's corners. From clothesline above, hang pot in frame at eye level.

Tie or tape rolls of wound newspapers to frame for legs. Hang folded newspapers over crossbar for face.

Wind dark crepe paper strips around animal's head and body. Fill pot with nuts, paper-wrapped candy, gum. Tape on newspaper lid.

Wind nose, ears, tail, legs and center with buff-colored crepe paper strips. Paste on circles for eyes and nostrils.

Weaver from Guatemala

Ukrainian egg decorator

Piper in Scotland

West Virginia glass blower

3

NEW INTEREST IN
OLD WAYS

Ethnic Reminders
from North to South

FROM ALASKA TO THE DEEP SOUTH, we have settlements of people descended from men and women who came from other continents.

Alaska's western tip is just fifty miles across the water from Siberia, which belongs to Russia. Here, thousands of years ago, the first Indians are believed to have come across the ice. Certainly, for centuries, only Indians and Eskimos lived in Alaska. Then, in 1741, a ship from Russia, navigated by a Danish seaman, stopped in Alaska and claimed this territory. From then, until 1867, when Russia sold Alaska to the United States for a little more than seven million dollars, only fur traders saw much value here. Then, gold was discovered, and American adventurers rushed in.

Today, the art of the Indians, Eskimos, Russians and early Americans tell us how people lived before Alaska became our forty-ninth state.

Travelers in every state find reminders of long ago settlers, but in some southern states, dozens of cultures are represented. Louisiana has known ocean pirates, Spanish explorers, French settlers, British soldiers, blacks, both slave and free, ragtime musicians, river pilots and some of the most romantic heroines in history. Here it was that Evangeline, heroine of Longfellow's epic poem, was said to have come from her home in Nova Scotia, when the British drove all the Acadians out. Legend says that long years later she and her love were reunited under an oak tree that still stands near St. Martinville.

In the far West, the stories are just as colorful. In Colorado's Indian settlements, the first Americans lived in their own apartments built into cliffs. In New Mexico's Santa Fe, the oldest capital city in the United States, the Palace of Governors (c. 1610) has flown Spanish, Mexican, Confederate and American flags. And in California, Indians and missionaries, cut-throats and preachers, prospectors and ladies of fashion, movie stars and hippies have come together at various times to build a state with a legend and an art form to match at every turn.

Feast bowls carved and inlaid years ago by Alaskan Indians are in Juneau's Alaska State Museum.

Russian Orthodox Church on Alaskan island has old icons and paintings. No pews—worshipers stand.

Early Spaniards carved this wall in back of altar in an old Santa Fe church.

Six hundred years ago, cliff dwellers lived in what is now Colorado.

Skills Learned from Others
Can Lead to Something New

This carved whale's tooth (scrimshaw), sometimes called "America's only true folk art," is the work of an American sailor. Note the American flag he has put on a ship, which is firing on another with a falling mast and holes in its sails. Today's engravers may use his methods, but may choose more modern subjects and more easily available materials.

Girl at Holland, Michigan, watching Dutchman make wooden shoes (called "klompen" because shoes make a klomping noise) may not want to make shoes, but she may do woodcarving.

This Greek wine jug at New York's Metropolitan Museum may inspire a potter to mold clay in a new shape. Or it may encourage an artist to work with a new shade of red. Or it may inspire a writer to weave a tale about Eros, the winged God of Love.

KOSHER SANTA CLAUS.
Santa Claus, jolly symbol
of holiday fun for Chris-
tian children, is repro-
duced in Israel in kosher
chocolate, to be enjoyed
during holidays by Jews.

NEW KIND OF PAPER SCULP-
TURE. Paper maharajah is
the work of Connecticut's
Ben Gonzales, a Philip-
pine-born sculptor, who
bends, folds and cuts paper
with a mat knife to make
original forms.

HERDING GOATS. This modern statue
of a Navajos Indian woman with her
goats was modeled by Allan C.
Houser, America's leading Indian
sculptor, who is a Fort Sill Apache
Indian from Apache, Oklahoma. The
model was duplicated in bronze (an
alloy of copper and tin) under the
direction of Mr. Houser, whose
Indian name Ha-oz-ous means "Pull-
ing Roots."

Only in This Country:
Art Forms from Everywhere

UNLIKE ARTISTS IN OTHER COUNTRIES whose backgrounds are much the same, American artists come from families that are nothing alike. And in their neighborhood, at schools and in museums, artists here can see work they admire by artists from countries they may never visit. This constant exposure to the art of people from other countries gives Americans an oportunity for diversity that is unique.

Each of these stoneware figures represents a point of the compass from which Americans have come. The foursome, reflecting the charm of children from the north, south, east and west, was made by Swedish artist, Lisa Larson.

Acknowledgments

Dancing the Highland Fling. The British Tourist Authority, New York City, page 3

Breaking a Mexican piñata. Mexican National Tourist Council, page 3

Hawaiian dance. Hawaii Visitors Bureau, Honolulu, page 3

Harry Zuber. Joan Zug, Amana Colonies, Iowa, page 4

Weaver. Travel and Promotion Division, Department of Conservation and Development, Raleigh, N.C., page 5

Carver. Idaho Division of Tourism and Industrial Development, Boise, page 5

Zoar calendar. Ohio Historical Society, Columbus, page 5

Gold double-headed pelican. Museum of the American Indian, Heye Foundation, New York, N.Y., page 6

Carved figure. University of Georgia Press, 1940. Photo by Muriel and Malcolm Bell, Savannah, page 7

Totem displays. Alaska State Museum, Juneau, page 7

Scrimshaw pie crimper. Donor H. H. Kynett, Mystic Seaport Photograph, Mystic, Ct., page 8

Billikins. Steve McCutcheon, Alaska Pictorial Service, Anchorage, page 8

Ivory walrus. Steve McCutcheon, Alaska Pictorial Service, Anchorage, page 9

Chinatown. New York Convention and Visitor's Bureau, page 10

Gold pendant figure. Museum of the American Indian, Heye Foundation, New York, N.Y., page 12

Gothic crown. Ministy of Information and Tourism, Madrid, Spain, page 13

Monstrance. Ministry of Information and Tourism, Toledo, Spain, page 13

Coin. Museum of the Casa de la Manedo, Madrid. Photo by Foto Mas, Barcelona, Spain, page 13

Gold Crown. Museum of the American Indian, Heye Foundation, New York, N.Y., page 14

Giraffe at Green Animals Park, Portsmouth. The Preservation Society of Newport County, Newport, R.I., page 16

Garden at Mount Vernon, Va. The Mount Vernon Ladies Association, Mount Vernon, Va., page 17

Girls from Java. Exxon Photo, page 86

Girl working; Repeat pattern; Butterflies and flowers. Exxon Photos, page 87

Helga Maurer Wagner and 2 pieces of her work, courtesy of the artist, page 88

Hokusai print. Metropolitan Museum of Art, Gift of Howard Mansfield, 1936, page 90

Origami face, #8 in series. Origami Center, New York, N.Y., page 91

Origami peacock by Adolfo Cerceda. Folded by Susan Heller. Origami Center, New York, N.Y., pg. 91

T'ang Dynasty horse. Avery Brundage Collection, Asian Art Museum of San Francisco, page 94

Musicians. The Metropolitan Museum of Art, Rogers Fund, 1923, page 95

Ancient bird. Art Institute of Chicago, page 96

"How to" with Sculptamold. Cle Knney, courtesy of American Art Clay Co., Inc. Indianapolis, Ind., page 97

Shoes in Morocco. Moroccan National Tourist Office, New York, N.Y., page 98

Mexican piñata celebration. Mexican National Tourist Council, New York, N.Y., page 104

Piper. British Tourist Authority, New York, N.Y., page 108

Weaver in Guatemala. David Vine, photographer, Brookfield Craft Center, Brookfield, Ct., page 108

Egg decorator. Courtesy Wasyll Gina, New Haven, Ct., page 108

Glassblower. West Virginia Department of Commerce, Charleston, W.Va., page 108

Feast bowls. Alaska State Museum, Juneau, page 110

Russian Orthodox Church on St. Paul Island, Alaska Tourist Bureau, page 110

Mesa Verde National Park. Colorado Department of Public Relations, page 111

Reredos in Santa Fe. Photo by Mark Nohl for the New Mexico Department of Development, Santa Fe, page 111

Girl watching man make wooden shoe. Michigan Tourist Council, Lansing, page 112

Greek wine jug. Metropolitan Museum of Art, Fletcher Fund, 1925, New York, N.Y., page 112

Whale's tooth. Mystic Seaport Photograph, Mystic, Conn. page 112

New kind of paper sculpture. Ben Gonzales, Bethlehem, Ct., page 113

Kosher Santa Claus. Nazareth Candy Co., Israel. page 113

"Herding goats." Photograph courtesy of the U.S. Department of the Interior, Indian Arts and Crafts Board, Southern Plains Indian Museum and Crafts Center, page 113

Children from One World. Rosenthal Studio-Haus, New York, N.Y., page 114

All other photographs were taken by Cle Kinney.